WEST GA REG LIB SYS
Neva Lomason
Memorial Library

THE WORLD'S GREATEST PLACES

THE MOST AMAZING TRAVEL DESTINATIONS ON EARTH

THE WORLD'S
GREATEST
PLACES

THE MOST AMAZING
TRAVEL DESTINATIONS ON EARTH

ABOUT THIS BOOK

To collect photography is to collect the world -
Susan Sontag

Human beings have become extremely mobile. It took Marco Polo years to reach the court of the Chinese Emperor, and Jules Verne journeyed "Around the World in 80 Days". Today, an airplane takes off every minute, unloading thousands of travelers on foreign continents in just hours. We visit the Antarctic, enjoy the beauty of Bali, go shopping in New York and Tokyo, stay in Dubai's luxury hotels, travel the Garden Route, dream of Hawaii, and sway along on the backs of elephants to visit the palaces of the last maharaja of Rajasthan. Human beings have been driven to travel the Blue Planet ever since Adam ate from the Tree of Knowledge – on a constant search for paradise lost and the most fascinating destinations in the world. But where do we find them?

More than anything, this World Travel Book is an invitation to get more familiar with the world and its magnificent natural and cultural treasures. Arranged geographically according to country, its pages present a selection of destinations – many of which are UNESCO World Heritage Sites – illustrated with images from the world's best photographers and featuring loads of background information. The result is a "world tour" to the most important, impressive and attractive places on earth.

To see, to dream...to travel. "The world is a book," wrote St Augustine, "and those who do not travel read only one page of it." We wish you an enjoyable journey...

Previous pages: the Golden Gate Bridge in San Francisco and Michelangelo's *David* in Florence.

St Lucia is often referred to as the "Helen of the West Indies". The mighty twin peaks of the Pitons on the south coast are the island's most famous landmarks.

EUROPE 10
ICELAND
Krafla, Godafoss, Dettifoss, Mývatn 12
NORWAY
Bergen, Geirangerfjord, Sognefjord 14
SWEDEN
Drottningholm, Stockholm 16
DENMARK
Copenhagen 18
FINLAND
Helsinki, Saimaa, Savonlinna, Koli 20
UNITED KINGDOM
London 22
Stonehenge and Avebury 24
Edinburgh 26
Highlands 28
IRELAND
Dingle, Beara, Iveragh, Killarney 30
NETHERLANDS
Amsterdam 32
BELGIUM
Bruges, Gent, Antwerp 34
FRANCE
Paris 36

Chalkstone cliffs of Normandy, Mont-Saint-Michel 38
Saint-Tropez, Nice, Cannes 40
Lubéron, Aix-en-Provence 42
Avignon, Marseille, Camargue 44
SPAIN
Barcelona 46
El Escorial, Madrid 48
Mallorca, Menorca, Ibiza 50
PORTUGAL
Lisbon 52
GERMANY
Berlin 54
Sylt, Föhr, Amrum, Helgoland, Wadden Sea 56
Munich 58
SWITZERLAND
Zurich, Bern 60
The Matterhorn 62
AUSTRIA
Vienna 64
Salzburg 66
ITALY
Rome 68
The Vatican 70
Venice 72
Pompeji 74
Sicily 76
POLAND
Gdansk, Torun, Frombork, Malbork 78
The Masurian Lake District, Białowieża 80
Krakow 82

CZECH REPUBLIC
Prague 84
HUNGARY
Budapest 86
CROATIA
The Plitvice Lakes 88
Dubrovnik 90
ROMANIA
The Danube Delta 92
GREECE
Athens 94
Delphi, Olympia, Epidauros, Mycenae, Soúnio 96
TURKEY
Istanbul 98
RUSSIA
Moscow 100
St. Petersburg 102

ASIA 104
SYRIA
Aleppo, Damascus 106
ISRAEL
Jerusalem 108
JORDAN
Petra, Wadi Rum 110
SAUDI ARABIA
Mecca, Medina 112
YEMEN
Sana'a, Schibam 114
UNITED ARAB EMIRATES
Dubai 116

IRAN
Isfahan 118
Persepolis 120
PAKISTAN
Karakoram 122
INDIA
Delhi 124
Agra 126
Jaipur 128
NEPAL
Kathmandu 130
NEPAL, CHINA
Mount Everest/Sagarmatha 132
RUSSIA
Kamchatka, Wrangel Island 134
CHINA
Beijing 136
The Great Wall of China 138
Shanghai 140
Hongkong, Macao 142
Tibet 144
JAPAN
Tokyo 146
Mount Fuji 148
VIETNAM
Halong 150
Ho-Chi-Minh City, Mekong Delta 152
CAMBODIA
Angkor 154
THAILAND
Bangkok 156
MALAYSIA
Kuala Lumpur, Batu Caves 158
Borneo 160

CONTENTS

INDONESIA
Bali and Lombok 162

AUSTRALIA/OCEANIA 164
AUSTRALIA
Simpson Desert, Uluru und Kata
  Tjuta, Nitmiluk 166
Great Barrier Reef 168
Sydney, Blue Mountains, Mungo 170
Tasmania 172
NEW ZEALAND
Tongariro, Egmont 174
Aoraki/Mount Cook, Westland 176
OCEANIA
Papua New Guinea 178
Fiji Islands,
  French-Polynesia 180

AFRICA 182
MAROCCO
Fez 184
Marrakesh 186
The High Atlas, Casbah Trail 188
TUNISIA
Kairouan, Tunis, El Djem 190
EGYPT
Cairo 192
Luxor, Karnak 194
Abu Simbel 196
MALI
The Niger, Timbuktu 198
KENYA
Amboseli, Tsavo, Maasai Mara 200

TANZANIA
Serengeti, Ngorongoro 202
Kilimanjaro 204
ZAMBIA/ZIMBABWE
Victoria Falls 206
BOTSWANA
Makgadikgadi, Okavango Delta,
  Chobe 208
NAMIBIA
Etosha 210
Namib Naukluft, Sossusvlei,
  Kokerboom Forest,
  Fish River Canyon 212
SOUTH AFRICA
Table Mountain, Cape Town 214
Winelands, Garden Route 216
MADAGASCAR
Madagascar 218
SEYCHELLES
Seychelles 220
MAURITIUS, FRANCE
Mauritius and La Réunion 222

THE AMERICAS 224
CANADA
Vancouver, Vancouver Island 226
Toronto, Niagara Falls 228
Montreal 230
UNITED STATES OF AMERICA
Alaska 232
San Francisco, Redwood 234
Yosemite 236
Las Vegas 238
Yellowstone 240

Bryce Canyon, Zion 242
Monument Valley 244
Grand Canyon 246
Chicago 248
New York City 250
Miami, Miami Beach,
  Florida Keys 252
Everglades 254
Hawaii 256
MEXICO
Mexico City 258
Campeche, Palenque 260
Uxmal, Chichén Itzá 262
BELIZE
Belize Barrier Reef 264
GUATEMALA
Antigua Guatemala, Tikal,
  Quiriguá 266
COSTA RICA
Costa Rica 268
COSTA RICA, PANAMA
Guanacaste,Cocos Island,
  Talamanca and La Amistad 270
CUBA
Havana, Viñales 272
VENEZUELA
Canaima 274
ECUADOR
Galapagos Islands 276
PERU
Machu Picchu 278
Cuzco 280
BRAZIL
Amazon Basin, Manaus 282

Rio de Janeiro 284
Iguaçu 286
BOLIVIA
Lake Titicaca, Altiplano,
  Cordillera Real 288
CHILE
Torres del Paine, Lauca,
  Alerce Andino 290
Atacama 292
Rapa Nui (Easter Island) 294
ARGENTINA
Buenos Aires 296
Los Glaciares 298
ANTARCTICA
Antarctica 300

LOCATION INDEX 302

Picture Credits/Imprint 304

Minakshi-Sundareshvara Temple in Madurai in the southern Indian state of Tamil Nadu possesses formidable dimensions. The complex is dedicated to the "fish-eyed" goddess Minakshi, Shiva's bride. Shiva is honored here as Sunarshvara, the "Beautiful God".

The fjords and cliffs of Scandinavia, the rolling forest landscapes of Central Europe, the snow-covered peaks of the Alps, the sun-filled shores of the Mediterranean, the legacy of the ancient Greeks and Romans, the monumental Medieval cathedrals, the magnificent baroque castles ... Europe! For Pope Boniface VII, Tuscany (here the Val d'Orcia) was in fact "the quintessence of the world".

KRAFLA

Situated just to the north-east of Mývatn, the countryside around Krafla, an active, 818-m (2,684-ft) volcano (above and main picture), is tectonically one of the least stable regions in Iceland. Believed for almost 2,000 years to be extinct, Krafla suddenly exploded to life at the beginning of the 18th century, smothering the region in a thick layer of lava and ash. What remained was a sparkling, emerald-green crater lake. In 1975 Krafla erupted yet again, this time for almost a decade. Its sulfur mud pots have been bubbling and steaming ever since. They are now a popular attraction as well as the most visible beacon of Iceland's continuing volcanic activity.

GODAFOSS

About 40 km (25 mi) to the east of Akureyri, traveling from the Sprengisandur gravel and lava desert toward the ocean, the Skjálfandaðfljót River thunders over a 10-m-high (33-ft) cleft in the terrain. The Goðafoss (right, top) owes its name, Waterfall of the Gods, to Thorgeir, speaker of the Althing, Iceland's parliament. In the year 1000, he is said to have thrown the statues of the former pagan gods into the river because the Icelandic parliament had decreed that Iceland should become Christian. The decision followed a threat from Norwegian King Olaf to stop the trade in timber, a move that would have endangered a vital industry for Iceland, shipbuilding.

DETTIFOSS

The Dettifoss (right) in Iceland's north-eastern corner is an impressive 100 m (328 ft) wide and 44 m (144 ft) high waterfall with a flow of up to 1,500 cu m (52,972 cu ft) per second, the most powerful in Europe.

The landscape surrounding the 818-m (2,684-ft) volcano just a few miles northeast of Lake Myvatn is one of the most tectonically unstable areas of Iceland.

MÝVATN

Roughly 30 km (17 mi) east of Goðafoss is "Mosquito Lake" (right), formed by the escaping lava from volcanic eruptions as recently as about 2,000 to 3,500 years ago. The lake covers an area of 37 sq km (14 sq mi) but it is only 4 to 5 m (13 to 16 ft) deep and fed by hot springs. Hardly anywhere else on the planet does such a diversity of fauna and flora exist at such northern latitudes. A great variety of mosses, grasses, ferns, herbs and birches grow along the lakeshore and on its numerous islands. During the summer months, huge swarms of mosquitoes buzz, giving the warm waters their name. Together with the insect larvae in the water, they provide nutrition for rich stocks of fish as well as several thousand waterfowl that nest in the network of bays.

The Mývatn also counts as one of Iceland's most spectacular landscapes due to its location in a zone of extreme volcanic activity. Strolling along the well-marked footpaths you will see an array of unusual lava formations. Especially bizarre are the Dimmu-borgir (Dark Castles), a series of fantastic formations that feature small caverns and arches.

You can get the best view of the pseudocraters in and around Mývatn from the rim of Hverfjall, an ash cone that rises roughly 170 m (558 ft).

Dalsnibba (1,476 m/4,843 ft) offers amazing panoramic views of the Sunnmøre mountain region (main picture) into which the Geirangerfjord slashes a more than 1,000-m-deep (3,281-ft) valley. You can also reach the mountain by car on a 5-km (3-mi) toll road.

BERGEN

From the 14th to the 16th centuries, it was mostly German merchants who controlled business dealings in the trading and port town of Bergen, Norway. The Germans ran the salt trade, an important ingredient needed to conserve the fish catches from the Norwegian Sea. In those days, salted fish was sold as far away as the Mediterranean and, thanks to its extensive commercial ties, Bergen eventually became one of the most important towns in the Hanseatic League.

On the Tyske Bryggen Quay – which means German Bridge and plainly reveals its use among Hanseatic merchants – gabled warehouses still bear witness to the former prosperity of this once mighty trading port. The 58 wooden houses that have been carefully preserved in the historic district, however, are not actually left over from medieval times. They were rebuilt in the original style after a fire in 1702. Fires have caused continuous damage in Bergen, which is still an important Norwegian port. The most recent fire was in 1955.

GEIRANGERFJORD

If statistics are proof, then the Geirangerfjord is one of the most impressive landscapes on the planet: The innermost arm of the Storfjord is roughly 120 km (75 mi) long and visited by more than 150 cruise ships from around the world each year. From the ship you will be able to see three famous waterfalls, among other things: Seven Sisters (above), Suitor and Bridal Veil. In summer, the Hurtigruten ships also dock in Geiranger, a village of about 250 people at the end of the fjord. The Ørneveien pass (or Eagle Road), from the Geirangerfjord to the Norddalsfjord farther north, is one of the most breathtaking roads in all of Scandinavia featuring hairpin turns and stunning vistas. The most spectacular viewpoint, however, can only be reached on foot at 1,112 m (3,648 ft) above the fjord: the nearly vertical Flydalshornet.

The Marina and the Old Town (left) are among the loveliest attractions in Bergen, Norway's second-largest city. Situated on the Byfjord, Bergen enjoys a mild climate as it is sheltered from the colder inland temperatures by mountains reaching up to 2,000 m (6,562 ft).

SOGNEFJORD

The Sognefjord (top) is not only Europe's longest fjord at 204 km (127 mi), but also the deepest on earth at 1,308 m (4,292 ft). Both Nærøyfjord (above left), flanked on both sides by rock cliffs up to 1,800 m (5,906 ft) high, and Aurlandfjord (above right) are arms at the south-eastern end of Sognefjord.

DROTTNINGHOLM

Completed in around 1700, Drottning-holm Palace (or Queen Island) is majestically located on Lovön Island in Lake Mälar, on the site of an earlier building dating back to the 16th century. Commissioned in 1662, by Hedwig Eleonora, wife of the late King Charles X Gustav, it is the largest baroque palace in Sweden and widely regarded as the most important work by architect Nicodemus Tessin.

The main façade of the rectangular structure faces the water. The palace was enlarged after 1750, and numerous rooms were furnished in the lavish style of the rococo. When the palace was increasingly used for state visits, starting in 1777, some of the important rooms were remodeled in elegant neoclassical style. King Gustav III (1771–92) had the gardens laid out in English landscape style.

Aside from the splendid rooms from a range of style periods, visitors are especially fascinated these days by the China Pavilion and the Drottning-holm Theater, one of very few rococo theaters still in use.

Royal Stockholm: the first Swedish regent, King Adolf Fredrick, moved into the castle (Kungliga Slottet) in 1754. Its 600 rooms making it one of the largest residences in the world (main picture).

Drottningholm Palace, residence of the Swedish royal family, is surrounded by several gardens and has been delightfully incorporated into the aquatic scenery around Lake Mälar (left).

STOCKHOLM

Founded in 1252, and the capital since 1634, Stockholm has long been a dynamic and international city, and its wonderful mix of grandiose buildings, parks, waterways and bridges give the vibrant metropolis a unique ambience.
All of the major sights can easily be visited on foot during a stroll through the Old Town (Gamla Stan), and overall there are roughly one hundred museums. In addition to the Nationalmuseet, which has the country's most important art collection, and the Moderna Museet, with contemporary art, it also features Skansen, the world's oldest open-air museum, and the Vasamuseet. The latter exhibits the Vasa, King Gustav II Adolf's flagship, which sank upon its launch in 1628.
The picture shows Riddarholmen Island with the steeple of Riddarholmskyrka church. This former place of worship is now a museum and the last resting place of the Swedish kings.

The sculpture of the Little Mermaid in the port of Copenhagen (main picture) was created by sculptor Edvard Eriksen based on the main figure in Hans Christian Andersen's fairytale. His models were the prima ballerinas who danced the part of the mermaid in a ballet interpretation of the fairytale, and his own wife.

NYHAVN

Since Denmark and Sweden were connected by the ambitious Öresund Bridge, it has become even easier to travel between the two "united kingdoms". One of the strangest, and yet somehow still accurate, travel recommendation for Denmark came from the much-loved and down-to-earth Queen Margrethe II: "No country is as much Denmark as Denmark itself." Indeed, it is an ideal travel destination for people who love the sea. Where else can you find 7,400 km (4,598 mi) of mostly undeveloped and freely accessible coastline combined with a choice of the blue shimmering Kattegat, the mild Baltic, the rough Skagerrak or the tidal North Sea?

And in Copenhagen, which has been the capital of Denmark since 1443, visitors encounter history and tradition around virtually every corner. The ambience is at once cosmopolitan and pleasantly tranquil, and

most of the sights can be comfortably visited on foot.

The city on the Öresund experienced its first period of prosperity back in the late Middle Ages as a trading port. A new golden age developed in the 16th and 17th centuries, in particular under King Christian IV, who did a lot to expand and further enhance the capital. The Nyhavn Canal district (above)

is particularly charming with its old wooden sailboats and a slew of cafés. Canal and harbor cruises begin here and take visitors to the popular Little Mermaid (Lille Havfrue, Copenhagen's most famous icon, main picture) on a rock in the bay. The statue was donated by Carl Jacobsen, a brewer and patron of the arts, and was finally unveiled in the year 1913.

AMALIENBORG

North of Nyhavn is the Amalienborg, city palace of Danish Queen Margrethe II commissioned by King Frederick V and completed between 1749 and 1760. It was based on designs by Nicolai Eigtved and has been the residence of the Danish royal family since 1794.

FREDERIKSKIRKE

Many visitors to Frederikskirke are reminded of St Peter's Basilica in Rome when they see its dramatic cupola (33 m/108 ft in diameter). Also known as the Marble Church, it was designed by Nicolai Eigtved, begun in 1749, and not completed until 1894.

CHRISTIANSBORG

Today, the Folketing, the 179-member Danish Parliament, holds its sessions in the former royal palace, which did not take on its present form until 1928. It was built on the site of two former structures, both of which were destroyed by fire.

HELSINKI

Roughly 500,000 people live in Finland's capital, a city originally founded by King Gustav I of Sweden in 1550. After a series of fires, Czar Alexander II commissioned Berlin architect Carl Ludwig Engel with the neoclassical reconstruction of Helsinki. Twenty of the monumental edifices from that time, 1820 to 1850, are still standing today and, along with other famous buildings in styles from Art Nouveau to modern, they lend the capital on the Gulf of Finland a unique urban landscape.

Worth seeing are Engel's Senate Square with the cathedral and the statue of Czar Alexander II (main picture), the Government Palace, the main university building and the university library, as well as the Orthodox Uspenski Cathedral, built in 1868 and boasting rich interior flourishes. Other attractions include the market square and the historic market building on the south side where the ferries dock that take visitors to the island fortress of Suomenlinna and the skerry islands. Numerous Art Nouveau buildings can be seen on Luotsikatu, one of Helsinki's most elegant streets. The esplanade, the capital's pedestrian zone, is bordered by parks. This is also where you will find Stockmann's flagship department store, the largest of its kind in all of Scandinavia.

The best panoramic view across Helsinki can be enjoyed from the Katajanokka Peninsula.

SAIMAA

With its countless fingers, bays and satellite lakes, the Saimaa region forms the largest connected lake district in Finland. Saimaa Lake itself (above, with Loikansaari Island) is also known as the "lake of a 1,000 islands". Up to 90 m (295 ft) deep in parts, it covers a vast area of about 1,300 sq km (502 sq mi), not including the islands. Spread out over several lakes is Savonlinna, the region's main town.

A statue of Czar Alexander II stands on Senate Square in Helsinki (main picture, with the 19th-century cathedral designed by the architect Carl Ludwig Engel in the background).

SAVONLINNA

Sights in the lovely little town of Savonlinna include the provincial museum, which is located in a former grain storehouse on Riihisaari Island in front of the gates of the castle; the converted museum ships "Mikko", "Savonlinna" and "Salama"; the market square with its docks for boat excursions into the Saimaa lake district; and the 100-year-old wooden villa Rauhalinna a short way outside of town.

Olavinlinna (above), an impressive fortress that can be reached via pontoon bridge, dates from the year 1475. It is considered Finland's most beautiful and most intact medieval castle complex. For more than thirty years it has played host to the Savonlinna Opera Festival, the country's largest regular cultural event.

KOLI

From the modest summit of this 347-m (1,139-ft) granite rise in Karelia, Ukko Koli, there are superb views of Lake Pielinen (above). Finnish artists saw the juxtaposition of granite rock formations, conifer and deciduous trees, and majestic lakes as a leitmotif of the Finnish natural landscape. Koli National Park invites you to explore its extensive hiking trails, but be careful of the national animal, brown bears (below).

LONDON

THE TOWER OF LONDON

During construction of the neo-Gothic Tower Bridge, the towers were clad with limestone from the Isle of Portland for aesthetic reasons as well as to hide the steel used in the bridge's substructure.

After his successful invasion of England in 1066, William the Conqueror commissioned the Tower of London as a fortified residence and observation post for the boats and barges plying the Thames. It was given its present appearance in the 13th century.

The Tower remained the royal residence of English monarchs until the year 1509, when the fortress was transformed into the state prison. Many famous citizens were held here, among them Thomas More, two of Henry VIII's wives, and the future Queen Elizabeth I.

The building is primarily a museum these days and has an extensive collection of European military items and torture devices. The Jewel House contains the crown jewels.

London's oldest church, the Norman Chapel of St John from 1080, is also on the grounds. Prisoners executed in the Tower, including two wives of Henry VIII (Anne Boleyn and Catherine Howard) and the Queen For Nine Days Lady Jane Grey, were buried in the St Peter Royal Chapel, restored in 1512 after a fire.

TOWER BRIDGE

Tower Bridge opened in 1894, and combines bascule and suspension bridge design. It is not only one of London's most famous landmarks, but is also an important testimony to the already advanced engineering capabilities of the time.

Originally, steam engines were used to operate the hydraulics, which allowed the bridge to be opened within just a few minutes. Today it is operated by electricity.

Both towers contain exhibitions on the structure's history, and from the glassed-in walkway high above the bridge you can get spectacular views of the city.

The castle complex, also known as the "White Tower" (left), is Britain's best-preserved fortress. With walls up to 3 m (10 ft) thick, it prevented breakouts as much as break-ins.

ST. PAUL'S CATHEDRAL

II's coronation in 2002. In 1981, Lady Diana Spencer and Prince Charles were married at St Paul's. Built between 1675 and 1710 on the site of a previous cathedral that was destroyed in the Great Fire of 1666, St Paul's is considered Christopher Wren's most important work.

St Paul's Cathedral rises above the city about 300 m (328 yds) north of the Thames. It is the main church of the Anglican Diocese of London and the venue for important state occasions, from the funeral of Lord Nelson in 1806 to the festivities celebrating the Golden Jubilee of Queen Elizabeth

FINANCIAL DISTRICT

London is one of the world's most important centers of business and finance. The prosperity of the city is reflected in its innovative architecture, for example in Richard Roger's Lloyd's building (above), which has all its service tracts, stairways and elevators on the outside of the structure.

The megaliths of Stonehenge near Salisbury are arranged in a circle of pillars connected by capstones (main picture). The stones of the inner circle came from the Preseli Hills in Wales, some 400 km (249 mi) away.

Stonehenge, an inspiring arrangement of megaliths in the county of Wiltshire, is still a mystery to us today. How were these giant stones transported? And what was the true purpose of the formation? The stones each weigh in at several tons and tower to heights of up to 7 m (23 ft) while an impressive trench 114 m (374 ft) wide surrounds the entire site.

During the final phase of construction, in roughly 2000 BC, the monoliths were transported hundreds of miles to this location, some having come from what is now Wales. They were then apparently oriented toward certain heavenly bodies, giving rise to the theory that the complex may have served both religious as well as astronomical purposes over the millennia.

The stone circle of Avebury east of Bath has the same orientation as Stonehenge and was built between 2600 and 2500 BC. According to an 18th-century British scholar, the Neolithic sanctuary was a druid temple, later destroyed under orders from the Church during the 1300s. Many of the megaliths were then used to build homes in the region.

The sun and the moon were probably the orientation points for the sanctuary at Stonehenge. Seen from the central altar stone, the sun once rose in between two sarsen stones, exactly aligned with the Heel Stone. Since then, it has shifted slightly with the gradual shift in the Earth's axis.

Of the former 154 stones at the Avebury site, only 36 have been preserved. Of those, 27 formed part of the large outer stone circle (left); they were inserted into the ground to a depth of 15 to 60 cm (6 to 24 in). In the 1930s, members of the National Trust began to re-erect the stones in their original positions.

EDINBURGH

Edinburgh Castle and the bell tower of the Balmoral Hotel are the main landmarks of the Scottish capital.

Edinburgh, the capital of Scotland, features a fascinating architectural contrast between the medieval Old Town and the carefully planned, Georgian-style New Town. The fortifications of Edinburgh Castle dominate the Old Town and date back to the 11th century. St Margaret's Chapel, consecrated in 1090, is also on Castle Hill. The Royal Mile descends from Castle Rock and is formed by Lawnmarket, High, and Canongate streets. It is the main thoroughfare of the Old Town and has numerous passageways and inner courtyards, elegant mansions such as Gladstone's Land, and various religious buildings such as the late-Gothic St Giles' Cathedral. At the eastern end of the Royal Mile is the Palace of Holyroodhouse, built in 1128 as an Augustinian monastery and later used as the residence of the Scottish kings. Opposite is the modern building of the new Scottish Parliament.

From top to bottom: Dugald Stewart Monument on Carlton Hill; the Old Town; the headquarters of the Bank of Scotland, crowned with a cupola and situated on a hill between Old and New Town.

BEN NEVIS

Ben Nevis rises majestically from the Grampian Mountains to a height of 1,344 m (4,410 ft), the highest mountain in the British Isles. It is one of 284 "munros", a name in Scotland given to mountains that are more than 3,000 ft (915 m) high and whose summits stand out noticeably from others. While the mountain's north-west slope is relatively easy for hikers to climb, the steeper north-east side, with its 460-m (1,509-ft) rock face is still a challenge even for experienced climbers.

GLENCOE

Glencoe is a beautiful and wildly romantic valley. A handful of its peaks, such as the Buachaille Etive Mór (top), rise above the 1,000 m (3,281 ft) mark.

RANNOCH MOOR

Rannoch Moor is the largest expanse of moorland in Great Britain and as such one of the last virtually untouched natural habitats in Europe.

Storm clouds gather at dusk above
Ben Nevis and Loch Eil.

DINGLE, BEARA, IVERAGH, KILLARNEY

Idyllic coastlines, picturesque villages, enchanting lake districts, steep cliffs, islands cloaked in myth and legend, remnants of ancient civilizations, and towns that are as historically exciting as they are vibrant – that is what awaits you in Munster, Ireland's largest province.

DINGLE

The Dingle Peninsula is the northernmost of five spits of land in County Kerry that point westward like fingers. With its gorgeous mountains, romantic rocky coast, and magnificent beaches it is one of Ireland's most beautiful and most popular regions. The mountains on either side of the Connor Pass, which at 456 m (1,496 ft) is the highest pass in Ireland, are a paradise for ramblers, while surfers will find excellent if cold conditions on the 5-km (3-mi) Surfer Beach near Inch on the peninsula's south coast.

Like everywhere in the west of Ireland, Dingle boasts relics of early Christendom. Especially impressive are the "beehive cells" of the early Irish hermit monks. In the early 6th century, Kerry's patron saint, St Brandon, allegedly prayed atop Mount Brandon (953 m/3,127 ft) before starting on his legendary journey to America in a curragh, a traditional sailing boat, with fourteen other monks. Mount Brandon is Ireland's second-highest mountain after Carrauntoohil, which checks in at 1,041 m (3,416 ft).

BEARA

Beara was the ancestral home of the O'Sullivans, the lords of Dunboy Castle near Castletownbere. When English troops took the castle in 1601, 1,000 clan members began a march across Ireland to the remote county of Leitrim; only 35 of them made it. Subsequent waves of emigration further reduced the population and today Beara is still a sparsely populated area.

In a bay near Castletownbere, the ruins of the Victorian Puxley Mansion are a reminder of the former copper mines of Beara. The home of a hated family of mine owners, it was burned down in the 1920 by the Irish Republican Army.

Right, top: The narrow road around the rocky Beara Peninsula offers superb views over more than 140 km (87 mi). Below that is a view of beautiful Ballydonegan Bay near Allihies.

IVERAGH

The drive around the Ring of Kerry takes you 170 km (106 mi) along the Iveragh Peninsula and is a highlight of any trip to Ireland. The ever-changing views of mountains and bays are simply breathtaking. A popular starting point for the tour of the Ring is Kenmare, a picturesque town with pastel-colored houses at the end of Kenmare Bay. Founded in 1775, Kenmare was known for its silk production.

Puffin Island (right) just off the west coast near the Bay of St Finan, is a popular nesting place for puffins, gannets and boobies.

Right, bottom: In a valley about 4 km (2.5 mi) from the south coast of Iveragh is the 2,000-year-old ring fort of Staigue. It once served as the residence of the kings of Munster and is today one of the best-preserved monuments of its kind in all of Ireland.

The Dingle Peninsula enchants with its wildly romantic coastal scenery (left). In the background is Mount Brandon shrouded in clouds. Behind it on the left, are the Three Sisters cliffs facing the opposite coast.

KILLARNEY

Ice Age glaciers formed the Killarney region, a mountainous lakeland area comprising more than 8,000 hectares (19,768 acres) near the town of the same name. Parts of the region have been made into a national park where the roads are free of cars. Any visit to the national park should include a trip by horse-drawn coach through the Gap of Dunloe, a mountain pass in the

On a swath of land near Lough Leane stands the late 15th-century Ross Castle (top).
Southwest of the town of Killarney is a region with three attractive lakes (middle, bottom and right).

shadows of Purple Mountain, which owes its name to the heather that flowers here in late summer. More demanding is the tour to the top of Carrauntoohil, Ireland's highest peak at 1,041 m (3,416 ft).
The oak and yew trees that grow in the park are fairly rare in Ireland, since most of the woods were cut down centuries ago. The strawberry tree is part of the unusual flora of the region, a shrub with red, edible fruits that normally only grows in the Mediterranean.

Tree masts were rammed as much as 30 m (98 ft) deep into the peaty ground to form the foundations of Amsterdam's Old Town. The result was not only seventy islands on stilts, but also the romantic ambience of a town on the water.

At the height of the "Golden 17th Century", construction began on the Three-Canal-Belt (left) whose half-moon shape includes the Keizersgracht canal (main picture). Four hundred bridges now crisscross the historic center alone, and the water level is kept constant with the help of a system of locks and pumps. Even commercial loads are still transported on the city's canals.

Hundreds of houseboats lie in anchor on the quays of Amsterdam's 160 waterways as well. They have become an iconic element of city life, just like the bicycles and the flower stalls selling "tulips from Amsterdam".

BRUGES

In the Middle Ages, the prosperous trade in textiles between England and the European continent went primarily via Bruges. Merchants from seventeen countries owned factories there. Thanks to generous patrons, Jan van Eyck and Hans Memling then transformed Bruges into a center of art and culture. Bruges reached its zenith in the 15th century when the dukes of Burgundy, active supporters of late-Gothic court culture, took up residence within its walls. International trade, however, soon began to decline when the river Zweyn silted up, thus blocking access to the sea.

The town, oval in its planning, is accessed by numerous canals and long streets with rows of gabled houses. These patrician mansions, the counting houses of the merchant princes, and the magnificent town hall (left) – where the counts of Flanders "liberated" the people – tell of the former prestige of the city. Its proudest icon is the belfry of the Cloth Hall (below)

GHENT

The city's most famous sights are nestled in the well-preserved historic heart of the city, between the Grafenburg and the 14th-century St Bavo's Cathedral, which is slightly elevated and visible from afar. Its greatest religious treasure is the famous "Ghent Altar" by the brothers Hubert and Jan van Eyck (15th century). The 95-m-high (312-ft) bell tower opposite the church was a symbol of the rising bourgeoisie in the 14th century.

Ghent, the capital of the Belgian province of East Flanders, is located at the confluence of the rivers Schelde and Leie.

ANTWERP

The lifeblood of Antwerp, Belgium's second-largest city, is its bustling port. An array of automotive and chemical companies are based there, and as one of the busiest ports in the world it has cultivated an atmosphere of openness to the world for centuries – a fact that has contributed significantly to the rise of Antwerp as a world center for diamonds.

Antwerp boasts a number of historic monuments and an exceptionally vibrant cultural life. Most of its sights are in the city center, which forms a semi-circle on the right bank of the Schelde. The most remarkable sight in Antwerp is probably the Steen, a former castle complex whose oldest parts date back to the 9th century. Today it houses the National Maritime Museum, which features a fascinating Flemish warship from the 15th century.

The castle's viewing platform offers superb views across the Schelde – more than 500 m (1,650 ft) wide at this point – of the bridges, the old quay, and the countless derricks scattered across the horizon down at the port.

PARIS

The French capital is steeped in history, and yet always ahead of the times. It is breathtaking in size, and yet seductive in its charm. One of few genuine world cities, Paris boasts a bewildering array of historic buildings and cultural landmarks.

Especially rich in history are the areas along the banks of the Seine, between Pont de Sully and Pont d'Iéna, beginning with the Île St Louis where the statue of Paris's patron saint stands, Ste Geneviève. Farther west, on the Île de la Cité, is the heart of Catholic Paris, with its Gothic Notre Dame Cathedral and Ste Chapelle, a filigree masterwork of High Gothic style.

Continuing along, opposite the Concièrgerie you come to one of the world's most important art museums, the Louvre. Farther down the Seine you arrive at the Musée d'Orsay, the Grand and Petit Palais, and the National Assembly. At the end of this stretch you reach the Eiffel Tower, a revolutionary steel structure completed in 1889 for the Exposition Universelle.

The Seine excursion boats, or "bateaux mouches," go right past the cathedral Notre Dame de Paris on the Île de la Cité in the Seine.

NOTRE DAME DE PARIS

Construction of the Gothic cathedral Notre Dame de Paris began on the Île de la Cité, an island in the Seine, in 1163. Among the new architectural elements were the transept and the rose windows, in the Rayonnant style (right), and the spectacular flying buttresses (main picture) on the east side of the church, each with a span of 15 m (49 ft). The main portal tympanum still features some of the original decoration, with figures portraying scenes from the Last Judgment. Notre Dame's interior is accentuated by five aisles with clustered columns and crossed-rib vaulting.

SAINTE CHAPELLE

Praised as a "miracle of the High Gothic," this former royal palace chapel was built in less than three years, presumably by Pierre de Montreuil, at the behest of King Louis IX. Comprising an upper (right) and lower (right, bottom) chapel, it represented a "gate to heaven" for the faithful in the Middle Ages. Thanks to nearly 360 degrees of 12-m-high (39-ft) stained glass windows, the Upper Chapel is a masterpiece of lighting that still mesmerizes visitors to this day. Completed in 1248, the chapel was to be a shrine for the holy relics that the pious Louis IX had bought (not "acquired") from the Emperor of Constantinople. In fact, he paid three times more for them than the entire cost of the chapel complex itself. These precious relics, which include the Crown of Thorns and a nail from Christ's Crucifix, are now kept in the treasury of Notre Dame.

CHALKSTONE CLIFFS OF NORMANDY, MONT-SAINT-MICHEL

On a rocky island out in the English Channel, in an exclusive spot about 1 km (1,100 yds) off the Normandy coast, is the former Benedictine Abbey of Mont-Saint-Michel, the most famous landmark in the region (main picture).

CHALKSTONE CLIFFS OF NORMANDY

It is not exactly delicate, this countryside stretching along the English Channel in the north-west of France. But the wind-battered coast and verdant green hinterland have their own undeniable magic that it is impossible to escape.

The Atlantic surf, the rugged shoreline, the gleaming white chalkstone cliffs and the long sandy beaches scattered in hundreds of bays along the spectacular Normandy coast present a nature full of brute force and primordial beauty. Strewn throughout the area are sleepy fishing villages and lively port towns as well as elegant seaside spas and pleasant holiday re-

sorts. The zenith of the Normandy chalkstone cliff landscape can be found at Étretat. This tiny fishing village was "discovered" by artists in the 19th century who thought it was particularly picturesque. Situated in a quaint cove, it is romantically framed by alabaster-white cliffs with bizarre rock formations that stretch along the steep coastline.

MONT-SAINT-MICHEL

The story of Mont-Saint-Michel began in the 8th century with the Vision of St Aubert: the Archangel Michael appeared before the bishop, and in return the bishop had a small prayer hall built for pilgrims.
In 1022, a new structure that incorporated the original walls was built atop the earlier church of Notre-Dame-sous-Terre. The crypt and choir, possibly the first choir ambulatory without radial chapels, were built first. After its collapse, the church was rebuilt in the late-Gothic style. In the 11th century, under Abbot Randulf of Beaumont, work continued on the crossing piers and transept, and the nave was completed at the beginning of the

12th century, under Abbot Roger I. The cross-ribbed vaults of the side aisles and central nave walls have been preserved only on the south side. The west front, with its twin towers, was completed in 1184, but burned down in 1776. People eventually settled at the

foot of the abbey and some houses from the 14th century are still standing. Due to driving sands and strong currents, Mont-Saint-Michel was difficult to reach even at low tide – it was besieged but never conquered.

The coast between Le Havre and Le Tré-port is known as the Alabaster Coast – Côte d'Albâtre – after its white chalk cliffs. In some parts, they reach more than 100 m (328 ft) in height. The eroded arch west of Étretat (left) is particularly famous; it resembles an elephant's trunk plunging into the water.

Cannes (main picture) is a popular stomping ground among the rich and famous, and one of the most glamorous towns on the Côte d'Azur. Luxury yachts line the port like pearls on a string.

NICE

This secret capital of the Côte d'Azur is a town full of contrasts. While the grand boulevards cling to memories of the Belle Époque, life in parts of Nice's Old Town resembles the scenes in a village in Italy.

The Greeks founded what they referred to as Nikaia, the "victorious town", in the 5th century BC, while the Romans preferred a location higher up in the hills for their settlement, Cemenelum, present-day Cimiez. The trademark icon of Nice is the Promenade des Anglais, built in the 1830s along the waterfront by wealthy English folks who

Top: The legendary Hotel Négresco adorns the eight-lane, 5-km (3-mi) seaside promenade in Nice.
Bottom: One of the most beautiful squares in the city, Cours Saleya.

had already recognized the benefits of Nice as a desirable place to retire in the mid-19th century.

The most impressive edifices from that period are the famous Hotel Négresco and the Palais Masséna. The Old Town features narrow, winding alleyways and houses with a distinctly Italian feel. The main square, Cours Saleya, has an attractive farmers' market. From the Castle Hill you can enjoy amazingly beautiful views of the Old Town and the Mediterranean.

SAINT-TROPEZ

Dense pine, oak and chestnut forests push their way down to the coastline between Fréjus and Hyères, two hills that drop off steeply toward the sea and leave no room for construction and development along the Corniche des Maures. The coastal road is all the more attractive thanks to this, winding along the wooded hills often half way up the incline and frequently offering superb views across the sea. In the numerous coves and bays, small former fishing villages huddle together having lost little of their original charm.

The motto in Saint-Tropez is to see and to be seen. The exclusive village first became famous through the film "And God Created Woman," which was shot here in 1956 by director Roger Vadim and featured his wife at the time, Brigitte Bardot. The idea of a decadent life by the sea first lured the youth of the world before the throngs of high-end tourists came rushing in. On her 40th anniversary, "BB" celebrated her retirement from cinema on the beach of Pampelonne just a couple miles from Saint-Tropez.

Jet-setters discovered the dreamy fishing village of Saint-Tropez (left) in the early 1950s. The town is said to have been named after a Roman soldier who had died a martyr's death as a Christian under Nero.

CANNES

The Celts and Romans had already established settlements around the Golfe de la Napoule in their times, but the bay did not become a popular destination until the 19th century, with the arrival of the British. Initially, they built beautiful villas for themselves before the upscale hotels followed. The Boulevard La Croisette was built around the entire bay.

Le Suquet, the Old Town, covers Mont Chevalier, a tiny hill that rises above the old port and whose summit is crowned by a watchtower dating back to the 11th century. Next to it, the Musée de la Castre displays relics from antiquity. The Gothic Notre Dame de

The luxury Carlton Hotel on the Croisette in Cannes.

l'Espérance dates from the year 1648. Magnificent views of the entire bay of Cannes unfold from the viewing platform behind the church, and on the edge of the Old Town is a giant hall that houses the Forville Market.

Cannes is of course also a town of festivals: the month of May is firmly set aside for the Film Festival, when the Golden Palm is awarded for the best film; in June, the international advertising industry meets in Cannes to select the best cinema and TV advertising spots; and in the fall, TV bosses from around the world gather there to buy and sell their programs. The venue for these activities is the Palais du Festival, at the western end of the Croisette.

The Abbaye de Sénanque (main picture) was founded by Cistercians in 1148, and had its heyday in the early 13th century before being destroyed in 1544. In 1854, seventy-two monks chanced a new beginning: Lavender fields now frame the abbey complex with its church and cloisters.

LUBÉRON

East of Avignon, halfway between the Alps and the Mediterranean, is the expansive limestone plateau of the Lubéron, a rocky landscape with lonely oak groves, small mountain villages and stone houses that has done well to preserve its impressive natural beauty. The mountains reach 1,125 m (3,691 ft) and contain some largely uninhabited stretches of land with more than 1,000 different species of plants. The "Parc Naturel Régional du Lubéron" was founded in 1977 to protect this unique environment.

The present-day isolation of many parts of the Lubéron is, however, deceptive – the limestone ridge, which was formed in the Tertiary period, has actually always been settled. The villages huddled in the hollows and valleys sprung up in the Middle Ages. Houses here have thick walls and churches served as both places of worship and refuge. The inhabitants of the Lubéron mostly depended on meager agriculture. When the harvests were no longer sufficient, the villages on the north side were abandoned.

AIX-EN-PROVENCE

In 122 BC, the Romans founded the hot springs colony of Aquae Sextiae Saluviorum on the ruins of the Celtic-Liguric settlement of Entremont. It later enjoyed the status of capital of Provence for centuries. During the Middle Ages, Aix first became an important center for the arts and learning after the 12th century.

The Old Town extends from the Cours Mirabeau, an avenue with

Developed as early as 1651, the Cours Mirabeau (top: Atlas on a house façade) forms the southern edge of the Old Town.

sycamore trees and beautiful city mansions from the 18th century, to the St Sauveur Cathedral, which has a baptistery dating back to Merovingian days. Other sights worth seeing are the 17th-century town hall, the Musée des Tapisseries and Paul Cézanne's studio. The favorite motif of the city's most famous son was Mont St Victoire to the east of Aix-en-Provence, which is worth a detour.

Flowering lavender fields are the trademark of Provence. Here, the proverbial "light of the south" is combined with beguiling scents and a riot of colors.

Camargue horses (main picture) have a compact build, slightly angular heads and a dense mane. The coats on these half-wild horses are not white until their fifth year.

AVIGNON

Catholic Church history was made in the 14th century in this southern French town on the Rhône: Between 1309 and 1376, the Roman Curia found refuge here from the political turmoil in Rome and went into "Babylonian exile." In 1348, Pope Clement VI bought the sovereignty of Avignon from Joan of Naples and it became the center of Christianity. Seven popes and later two antipopes resided here in the roughly 100-year period that eventually led to the Western Schism.

The papal residence consists of an Old and a New Palace. On the north side is the 12th-century Roman cathedral Notre Dame des Doms. Also part of the bishops' district is the Petit Palais, built in 1317, which was intended to compensate the archbishop for the demolition of his original palace.

From the 14th century, Avignon was surrounded by an imposing town wall that was strengthened with fortified towers such as the Tour des Chiens and the Tour du Châtelet. The latter controlled access to the world-famous Pont d'Avignon.

MARSEILLE

France's second-largest city and the most important port in the country, Marseille boasts more than 2,500 years of history. Its importance as a major gateway for incursions into North Africa is also mirrored in the composition of its population.

The town of Massalia was originally founded by Greeks from Asia Minor on the hill where Notre Dame de la Garde stands today. Initially Rome's allies, it was not until 49 BC that Caesar finally conquered the Greek republic. The port town experienced its first major period of prosperity in the 12th century when armies of crusaders brought lucrative business to the city for their trips from Marseille to Jerusalem. In the centuries

Notre Dame de la Garde watches over the port of Marseille.

that followed it was the most important port in the Mediterranean.

Today, the heart of Marseille still beats in the old harbor. It is from there that La Canebière, the city's main boulevard, starts its way through the entire city. It was once the symbol of a vibrant city with a penchant for extravagance. The entrance to the port is flanked on the north side by Fort St Jean and on the south side by Fort St Nicolas.

The basilica Notre Dame de la Garde is Marseille's most enduring landmark and is visible from quite a distance. The square in front of it, the Plateau de la Croix, affords the best views of the port and city. Another excellent vista point across the water to Marseille is from the summit of the Château d'If rock.

Also worth seeing are the St Victor Basilica, Notre Dame de la Garde, Château d'If on a rocky island offshore from the port, and the Citadel.

View of Avignon, capital of the Département Vaucluse, from the opposite bank of the Rhône. Only four original arches remain of the much-celebrated Pont St Bénézet bridge (left). The medieval city is surrounded by 4.5 km (3 mi) of heavy fortifications.

CAMARGUE

The estuary between the two main distributaries of the Rhône comprises 140,000 hectares of swamps, meadows and grazing land as well as dunes and salt marshes – it is one of Europe's largest wetlands. Agricultural use, mostly for the cultivation of rice, is concentrated in the northern part of the Camargue; in the south-eastern portion salt is harvested in shallow lagoons. The south, however, is a nature paradise unique in Europe, with half-wild horses, bulls, and aquatic birds and waders.

The grassy meadows of the estuary are a home to the Camargue horses (top) as well as to many waterfowl and waders: about 10,000 pairs of flamingos (bottom) breed here.

More than 350 species of migratory bird stop at the "Parc Ornithologique du Pont-de-Grau" in the south-west of the Camargue. The main distinctive feature of the black Camargue bulls are their lyre-shaped horns. The white horses of the Camargue were even depicted in the ancient cave paintings of Solutré. When trained to take saddle and tack, they are untiring companions and can be of great service for herding livestock. A number of operators also offer guided excursions on horseback even for inexperienced riders that lead into the swamps, out to the beaches and to see the bulls. They allow you to see some of the normally less accessible parts of the Camargue to be enjoyed.

BARRI GÒTIC, LA RAMBLA, PLAÇA DEL REI, LA BOQUERIA

Barcelona, bustling metropolis with 1.7 million inhabitants, is the capital of Catalonia and for some the true capital of Spain. A Mediterranean city, it has a romantic Old Town as well as a New Town with wide boulevards that invite strollers and shoppers. The city has a lively history: Hannibal's father is said to have originally founded it, and it eventually became an important stronghold for the Romans. During the Middle Ages it was in the hands of the caliph of Córdoba before becoming the residence of the kings of Aragón. Today, Barcelona is a city of culture, industry and trade. The Barri Gòtic, the Gothic Old Town, invites you to wander the alleyways; la Rambla leads down to the port where a monument to Columbus has been erected. On the medieval Plaça del Rei is the palace of Catalan and Castilian kings. The nostalgic La Boqueria market presents an overwhelming selection of goods.

PALAU DE LA MÚSICA

The Palau de la Música Catalana (Palace of Catalan Music) is the most important concert hall in Barcelona. Designed by Domènech i Montaner in 1908 for the "Orfeo Catalá" chorus, the steel frame of this Art Nouveau building is clad in shiny, colorful materials, including ceramics and stained glass. Some famous artists of the Catalan Art Nouveau style joined in the design of the interior as well, making the harmonious combination of light and space a particularly impressive element. Also noticeable are the lavish flowers and climbers ornamenting the ceiling, walls and columns of the hall along with dragons' heads and other sculptures.

LA SEU

In the very heart of the Barri Gòtic is Barcelona's cathedral, which dates from the 14th century. Following a very long tradition, geese are the guardians of the graves in its cloisters.

The Art Nouveau style is embodied in a special way by the Sagrada Familia (main picture), which features spindly turrets and organic shapes inspired by nature.

SAGRADA FAMILIA, PALAU GÜELL, PARQUE GÜELL, CASA MILÀ, CASA BATLLÓ, CASA VICENS, COLONIA GÜELL

Architect Antoni Gaudí i Cornet is considered an outstanding representative of Modernism, or Catalan Art Nouveau. He created some of his most magnificent buildings in Barcelona such as the Sagrada Familia (main picture), a church that was originally designed in the neo-Catalan style in 1882,

and which has still not been completed. For Eusebi Güell, a generous patron of the arts, Gaudí designed an idiosyncratic city mansion, the Palau Güell, which was completed in 1889 after four years of construction. Typical for the artist, ornamentation and organic forms dominate here.

The Parque Güell was conceived as a small garden city. Although the park was created according to detailed plans from 1900 to 1914, it seems to have grown naturally. The Casa Milà (left), built between 1905 and 1911, is a multi-story apartment block whose bizarre design makes it hard to distinguish architecture and sculpture. The Casa Batlló (right) is a magnificent city mansion with a roof designed by Gaudí to represent a large dragon and adorned with mosaic chimneys. For the interior design of the Casa Vicens, Gaudí adapted some ideas from Mudéjar architecture. Of the Colonia Güell Church, he was only able to complete the crypt, but a drawing by the master exists that gives you an idea of how the structure was supposed to have looked in its final form.

EL ESCORIAL

In 1561, eager to express his hunger for power and bolstered by his successes in the war against France, Philip II commissioned the construction of a vast palace in Escorial, some 60 km (37 mi) north-west of Madrid. The original architect was Juan Bautista de Toledo; after his death, Juan de Herrera took over in 1567, supervising construction until near completion in 1584. The rectangular complex (above) covers a vast area of more than seven acres and provides space for sixteen courtyards. It is equipped with nine towers.

The composition of the buildings was inspired by the Temple of Jerusalem, and thanks to its perfect symmetry it remained for a long time the prototype for many other extravagant palaces across Europe.

The magnificently furnished royal mausoleum houses the remains of all Spanish monarchs since Philip II. In addition to the countess private and staterooms of the royal family, the comprehensive library (main picture) is an impressive feat that contains many priceess volumes.

MADRID

The capital of Spain is not only the geographic heart of the Iberian peninsula, but it was at one point also the center of an empire in which "the sun never set." Over centuries, dynasties such as the Habsburgs and the Bourbons each left their own mark on the city. Accordingly, the cityscape is wildly diverse even in the center. Since the end of the Franco dictatorship in 1975, Madrid has undergone a rapid change and developed from a sleepy administrative town into a pulsating world city.

As the capital, Madrid has been a big draw for artists and merchants since the 16th century. Velazquez and Goya were invited as painters to the Spanish royal court, during which time they created some of their famous masterpieces. A com-prehensive collection of paintings from them and other artists can now be admired in the Museo del Prado, one of the most famous classical collections in the world. It comprises more than 9,000 works of art including Goya's 1814 piece *The shooting of the rebels on May 3, 1808* (above), 5,000 illustrations and 700 sculptures. The capital naturally has a wealth of other world-renowned museums as well. In terms of its architecture, Madrid features a great variety of styles ranging from the Renaissance in the "Madrid de los Austrias" district (for example, the Monasterio de las Calzas Reales, right) to the baroque and neoclassicism in the Palacio Real (top) and a range of Art Deco and postmodernist edi-fices around town. The impressive main square of the city – and the model for many other Spanish squares – is the 17th-century Plaza Mayor (top left with the equestrian statue of Philip III). San Francisco el Grande (left bottom) is a domed church built in 1770 on the site of an earlier Franciscan monastery and holds important paintings by Goya, Velázquez and others. Documentation shows that a church was built as early as the 9th century where today the Nues-tra Señora de la Almudena Cathe-dral (top right) stands. Incidently, the cathedral was not consecrated until 1993, after more than 100 years of construction.

Steep cliffs are typical of the Cap de Formentor in the north-east of Mallorca. Wind and water have created a spectacular coastline here.

MALLORCA

"If you like Paradise," wrote Gertrude Stein, "Mallorca is paradise." Every year, this Mediterranean island is visited by millions of tourists, and yet it still has some quiet bays and breathtaking landscapes. Mallorca is an island like an entire continent, with wilderness and surprisingly high mountains in the north, vast almond plantations and cornfields in the interior, and miles and miles of beaches and coves in the south. A holiday paradise with an area of 3,640 sq km (1,405 sq mi) and surrounded by turquoise seas, its capital Palma (right center with the La Seu Cathedral towering high above the port) is the most prosperous town in

Spain by gross national product. And those who wish to escape the bustle of the coastal resorts between Andratx and Arenal, and discover the beauty of nature and meet the people in the small villages, will only have to go a short way inland. The mountain village Valldemossa (right bottom), for

example, boasts a charterhouse whose monks' cells were converted into small apartments in the 19th century. In 1838/39, Frédéric Chopin and George Sand lived there, a fact that has attracted music lovers from around the world ever since. Near the Port de Valldemossa is the majestic Son

Marroig (far left top), former summer residence of the Austrian Archduke Ludwig Salvator on the "Costa Brava Mallorquina." An excursion to Cap de Formentor, the northernmost point of this spectacular island, is indeed breathtaking (above and main picture).

MENORCA

IBIZA

Covering an area of 716 sq km (276 sq mi), Menorca is only about one-fifth the size of Mallorca. And it is this fact to which it owes its name, Menorca (the "smaller one"). "La Isla verde y azul", or "the island of blue and green", is divided into two regions named after the prevailing north and south winds: the Tramuntana in the north and the Migjorn in the south. The border between these two regions, which are very different geologically, runs along the road from Maó (above), the island's capital, to Ciutadella (top right). Around sixty per cent of the roughly 87,000 people on Menorca live in these two towns. It is the least densely inhabited island in the archipelago with less than ten per cent of the total Balearic population.

The Cala Macarelleta (below) is one of Menorca's paradisical bays. Many visitors come by boat and drop anchor in the bay, which can only be reached via footpath.

Ibiza and Formentera form the western end of the Balearic Islands, which together form an autonomous region (and province) of Spain. High above the steep coast at Cap Jueu on the south-western tip of the island, you can see the uninhabited islands of Vedranell and Es Vedrá from the "Torre del Pirata".

Eivissa, the official Catalan name for Ibiza (above) is the island's main town, administrative center and also a bishops' see. Though it is most famous for having the most lively party scene and night-clubs in the Mediterranean, Ibiza also has an imposing fortress in the upper town.

TORRE DE BELÉM

The richly adorned tower of Belém (main picture) was built in 1521 on the orders of Manuel I as a watchtower to protect the Tagus estuary, the location where Portuguese sailors once embarked on their journeys of exploration. With its many balconies and battlements, Belém is an impressive example of Manueline architecture and also one of Lisbon's most famous landmarks.

The massive multi-story building, which in later periods served as both a weapons arsenal and a state prison, displays Moorish, Gothic and Moroccan influences. Its grand presence was meant to welcome home the captain and crew of richly loaded ships and at the same time, because of its similarity with a ship's bow, persuade potential enemies that the armada had left the harbor for a counterattack.

Over centuries, the Tagus silted up so much that the tower today no longer stands at the estuary but on the riverbank. There are superb views from the highest platform at 35 m (115 ft).

ALFAMA, BAIRRO ALTO, BAIXA

A sea of houses climbs from the wide estuary of the river Tagus up the steep hills of the "white city". Lisbon, the capital of Portugal, has a superb location that attracts visitors from around the world who, like the locals, travel aboard the city's "eléctricos", rickety old trains that squeak their way through town.

Particularly worth seeing is the Alfama, Lisbon's oldest and most picturesque neighborhood, a labyrinthine Old Town on Castle Hill, which is crowned by the ruins of the Castelo de São Jorge. Between the castle ruins and the medieval Sé Cathedral are two of many miradouros, attractive viewing platforms that Lisbon is famous for and from which you can enjoy spectacular views across the city. Author Fernando Pessoa, a native of Lisbon, said of his city there exists "no flowers that can match the endlessly varied colors of Lisbon in the sunlight.". Lisbon is divided into an upper town (the bairro alto) – the entertainment quarter with its lively pubs, traditional restaurants and fado bars – and a lower town (the baixa), which was rebuilt after the devastating earthquake of 1755 according to the city's original plans and is today the banking and shopping district.

The best view of the baixa can be enjoyed from the Elevador de Santa Justa, a cast-iron lift between lower and upper town that was built in 1901 (left).

Belém is an abbreviation for Bethlehem. Once equipped with canons, the Torre de Belém still watches over the port and recalls the age of the great seafarers and explorers (main picture).

HIERONYMITE MONASTERY

tery on the site where the Infante (Prince) Henry the Navigator had earlier built a chapel. The plan for the overall complex dates back to Master Boytac and the column-less transept is a late work by João de Castilho. An impressive testimony of contemporary statuary is the sculpted decoration in the church's south and west portals. The spectacular church itself (left), a hall church with late-Gothic and early-Renaissance styles, measures 92 m (300 ft) in length and 25 m (85 ft) in width.

Many important figures from history were buried in the Hieronymite Monastery. It holds, for example, the tomb of Vasco da Gama (below, the sarcophagus), whose discovery of the sea route to India secured the finance for furnishing the monastery.

Emanuel I the Fortunate, king of Portugal from 1495 to 1521, was an avid supporter of the country's maritime explorations, in particular those of Vasco da Gama and Pedro Cabral, credited with the discovery of the sea route to India and Brazil, respectively. Indeed, during his reign, the arts and sciences flourished. To honor Vasco da Gama, in 1502, he commissioned the enormous Hieronymite Monas-

KURFÜRSTENDAMM

"Great Berlin, the open city – it should not be just a German city," wrote Mexican author Carlos Fuentes, before adding, "It is our city, a city of the whole world." And in fact, Berlin stands at the heart of the world like virtually no other city. History was, and still is, made in this city on the river Spree, and the past and the present connect with whatever the next future may be. As the capital and seat of government, home to muses and museums, and as a multicultural center, Berlin is a city like no other. Or more precisely: "a city of the whole world."

The capital of the German Empire should have a grand boulevard modeled after the Champs-Elysées in Paris. That was the decision by Chancellor Otto von Bismarck upon his return from the French capital after the Franco-Prussian War. And so the former corduroy road to the hunting palace in Grunewald forest was transformed into a 3.5-km (2-mi) long, 53-m (174-ft) wide avenue where only those who could afford it lived. Today, the shops here compete with the up-and-coming Mitte (center) district, but as a shopping street, Kurfürstendamm (above) is still number one in Berlin.

Two warriors guard the forecourt of Charlottenburg Palace with its equestrian statue of the Great Elector Friedrich Wilhelm (main picture).

SCHLOSS CHARLOTTENBURG

In the heart of the Charlottenburg district and originally conceived as a summer residence for Electress Sophie Charlotte, this grandiose edifice was built in several stages between 1695 and 1746. The domed tower rises almost
50 m (164 ft) above the palace forecourt with its equestrian statue of the Great Elector. After World War II, the historic rooms in the central building – the oldest part of the complex, which also comprises extensive palace gardens – were rebuilt in their original splendor.

KAISER WILHELM MEMORIAL CHURCH

"Everything passes" was the main theme of the sermon in the Kaiser Wilhelm Memorial Church on November 22, 1943. It was the last Sunday before Advent, commemorating the dead. Bombs soon after reduced the church to the now famous ruin (above, through the sculpture "Berlin" in Tauentzien Street). The damaged west steeple, reduced from 113 to 63 m (371 to 207 ft), was then given the nickname "hollow tooth" by locals. Despite their irreverence, however, Berliners did not allow the destroyed church to be demolished and in 1961, Egon Eiermann built a monument church over the ruins.

SYLT

Sylt, known for its see-and-be-seen ambience, is the northernmost island in Germany. At the northern tip of the island is the tiny community of List, the northernmost place in the republic. Sylt splitt off from the mainland some 8,000 years ago when the seas began rising. In 1927, the two were linked again by the Hindenburgdamm.

Since then, up to 650,000 holiday-makers a year cross the dam to the 39-km-long (24-mi) island which, at its widest point is just over 1 km (0.6 mi) wide. While the west coast is lashed by the wind and the waves of the North Sea, the eastern Wadden Sea coast is much quieter and calmer. It is also home to Wadden Sea National Park, famous for its diversity of flora and fauna as well as its tidal mud flats.

FÖHR

Christian VIII, King of Denmark and Norway, had already discovered the beneficial effects of the fresh air, beautiful scenery and the almost 15 km (9 mi) of sandy beaches in the south of the island of Föhr back in the middle of the 19th century. The center of the nearly circular island, 82 sq km (32 sq mi) in size, is the North Sea resort of Wyk.

The west and south of Föhr was formed by a moraine – a glacial relic from the Ice Age. It is higher and drier than the marshlands of the north and east, which only gradually grew with increased land reclamation.

AMRUM

South-west of Föhr lies the quiet island of Amrum, about 20 sq km (8 sq mi) in size and featuring dunes up to 30 m (98 ft) high. Amrum also has a sandy beach that is up to 2 m (1.3 mi) wide and 15 km (9 mi) long – the famous Kniepsand beach. The small island has a population of roughly 2,200 people living in five villages, of which the Friesian village of Nebel is the best known and most popular. To get an good view of the island with its dunes, forests and marshlands, it is best to climb the 66-m-tall (217-ft) lighthouse between Nebel and Wittdün. From there you can see the entire island and sometimes as far as neighboring Föhr.

HELGOLAND

You have to catch a boat if you want to visit Helgoland, with its famous buntsandstein (red sandstone) formations and breeding grounds for guillemots and kittiwakes. Germany's only solid rock, high-seas island was actually in British hands for many years before becoming German in 1890, when it was swapped for the island of Zanzibar. During World War II, Helgoland was a military base, and as such was frequently bombed. After the war, the island was used as a bombing range by the British but by 1952 it was given back to Germany and by the mid-1950s, the first inhabitants had begun returning to the island, rebuilding their lives, and welcoming the first visitors, who came to enjoy the fresh air and duty-free shopping. Daytrippers still arrive in large numbers.

SCHLESWIG-HOLSTEIN – WADDEN SEA

The Wadden Sea is an annual stop-over for more than two million migratory birds as well as a summer retreat for about 100,000 breeding shelducks, eider ducks, seagulls and swallows. In addition, the tidal area is a breeding ground for herring, sole and plaice as well as a habitat for gray seals, harbor seals and harbor porpoises.
In an area covering more than 4,000 sq km (1,544 sq mi), from the Danish border to the estuary of the river Elbe, Wadden Sea National Park provides more than 3,000 different animal and plant species with an ideal environment. Schleswig-Holstein was the first German state to place the northern stretches of the Wadden Sea under protection, declaring it a national park in 1985, and then a biosphere reserve in 1990. The Wadden Sea National Park is divided into three protection zones. The first zone includes the seal colonies, where humans are either not allowed at all, or only allowed on designated paths. Part of the second zone is the whale protection area. The third zone is open to fishing, tourism and even oil drilling.
The Wadden Sea is a perfect ecosystem that is rich in nutrients. Many animal and plant species have even adapted to living in the salt marshes, the best-known among being is the lugworm.

An estimated 10,000 lighthouses still exist around the world, and some of the most attractive ones can be found on the German North Sea coast. This one stands on the Ellenbogen Peninsula, the northernmost tip of the island of Sylt.

MUNICH

Founded in 1158, Munich owes much of its meteoric rise to Napoleon, who in 1806 made Munich the capital of Bavaria. King Ludwig I brought architectural splendor to the city while his son Maximilian II promoted the arts. The Alps seems to begin just beyond the city limits (main picture).

THE RESIDENZ

The Residenz is the historical seat of power in Munich and it is from here that Bavaria's counts, electors and kings ruled. It was built in the 16th century to replace the Neuveste Castle (from the 14th), which had replaced the Old Court as the ducal seat. Between 1568 to 1619, a Renaissance complex was built that was later expanded to include baroque, rococo and neoclassical styles.

Since World War II, the Residenz now comprises ten courtyards and 130 rooms. The Court Church of All Saints as well as the former Residenz Theater (now the Cuvilliés Theater), a splendid, newly restored rococo building, are also part of the complex.

The Residenz still plays an important role in Munich. It houses museums (including the Porcelain, Silver and Treasure Chambers in the Königsbau, Cabinet of Miniatures, State Collection of Coins, Collection of Egyptian Art) and is a prestige building for festive occasions and receptions, for example in the Antiquarium, the largest Renaissance hall north of the Alps.

MARIENPLATZ

Munich's urban center is framed by the neo-Gothic New Town Hall from 1909 (above) with its famous Glockenspiel, as well as the Old Town Hall from 1480. When Ludwig the Bavarian granted the market charter to Munich in 1315, he stipulated that the Marktplatz remain "free from building for all eternity". In 1638, Elector Maximilian I had the Marian Column erected there in gratitude for the city being spared during Swedish occupation in the Thirty Years' War. Since 1854, the center of Munich has been known as Marienplatz, named after the Madonna on top of the column.

FRAUENKIRCHE

The onion domes of the Frauenkirche are the most recognizable icons of Munich, the capital of Bavaria. They also mark an important limit: no building in the city center can be higher than their 99 m (338 ft). The Church of Our Lady, more accurately called "Cathedral of Our Blessed Lady", has ten bells. Susanna, the largest bell, dates back to 1490, and weighs eight tons. Built in what would have been a record time of twenty years by Jörg Halspach, the Gothic church is 109 m (358 ft) long, 40 m (131 ft) wide, and accommodates roughly 20,000 people. It has been the cathedral church of the archbishops of Munich and Freising since 1821.

The Antiquarium (far left, 1568–1571) is the oldest preserved room in the Munich Residenz. The name refers to the antique sculptures that decorate the space. The Cuvilliés Theater (left) is the most attractive loge theater of the Rococo age.

HOFBRÄUHAUS

Hundreds of visitors from around the world stream in and out of the Hofbräuhaus on a daily basis. It accommodates up to 1,300 guests and has become a venue of cultish proportions. The beer hall goes back to 1589, when Duke Wilhelm V had a brewery built to supply his court and servants. In 1828, Ludwig I began selling the beer at prices soldiers and working class people could afford, so they too could enjoy this "healthy" drink. The most famous regular here is an angel, Alois Hingerl, from Ludwig Thoma's 1911 story "Ein Münchner im Himmel". After too many beers he forgot his task and still sits there to this day.

NYMPHENBURG

In 1662, Electress Henriette Adelaide bore her husband, Elector Ferdinand Maria, a son and long-awaited heir to the throne of Bavaria, Max Emanuel. To show his gratitude, the ruler gifted her the extravagant Nymphenburg Palace. Unfortunately, she would not live to see its completion in 1757.
The palace's baroque façade is 700 m (766 yds) wide. Behind that, the palace park covers over 3 sq km (1 sq mi), with greenhouses, the Badenburg and Pagodenburg pavilions, and the Amalienburg hunting lodge. The summer residence of the Wittelsbachs and birthplace of Ludwig II, Nymphenburg boasts stately rooms, the Gallery of Beauties, a Nymphenburg Porcelain exhibit, and the Museum of Carriages and Sleighs in the former royal stables.

Magnificent city gates and arcades are the landmarks of Bern's historic city center. The main picture shows the view along the Kramgasse and the Marktgasse to the Käfigturm (Prison Tower) and Zytgloggeturm (Clock Tower).

ZURICH

It is a cliché, and an incorrect one at that, to assume that the country's economic metropolis on Lake Zurich, with its more than 100 banking headquarters, is just a boring, old-fashioned financial center. Zurich boasts numerous architectural gems such as the Fraumünster church in the Old Town west of the river Limmat , which has a set of five windows by Marc Chagall. Next door is the 13th-century parish church of St Peter with Europe's largest clock face. The Grossmünster on the other side of the river, its neo-Gothic tower cupolas dominating the cityscape, entered the annals of church history as the domain of the reformer Huldrych Zwingli (1484–1531).

BERN

Once the largest city-state north of the Alps, Bern's historic center clearly depicts the chronological order of its different periods of expansion. The stately guild and townhouses with arcades extending for a total of 6 km (4 mi) are characteristic of the city center. Construction of the late Gothic St Vincent Cathedral began in 1421 and was only completed in 1573; the magnificent main portal was designed by Erhard Küng. The late-

The highly expressive Pfeiferbrunnen Piper's Fountain) in Bern.

Gothic townhouse was erected between 1406 and 1417 and renovated in 1942. The Heiliggeistkirche (Church of the Holy Spirit), from 1729, is one of the country's most important examples of Protestant baroque architecture. Bern's landmark, however, is the Zytgloggeturm (Clock Tower) city gate.

The ensemble of lovely historic residential buildings in the Gerechtigkeitsgasse stands out from the multitude of beautiful buildings in Bern, and some of them date back to the 16th century. Bern's Renaissance fountains with their lovely expressive figures are also worth seeing, three of them having been created by the Freiburg sculptor Hans Gieng.

The twin towers of Zurich's Grossmünster dominate the skyline of this, the "smallest large city in the world", situated at the northern end of Lake Zurich seen with the river Limmat – a tributary of the Aare – running through it (far left and left).

Enchanting in shape and with a magical light, it is no wonder that the Matterhorn is also referred to as the "crown jewel of the Alps". A particularly lovely view is with Riffel Lake in the foreground (main picture). The normal route up to the 4,478-m (14,692-ft) summit is via the distinctive Hörnligrat.

What hasn't already been written about this mountain! Bombarded regularly with superlatives, the Matterhorn's incomparable shape is much vaunted, having been referred to as the "advertising mountain" due to its use in promoting just about everything.

Who would have thought? The Matterhorn adorns not only Swiss yoghurt containers and Belgian beer bottles, it has also found itself on wine labels and on Japanese confectionery, on a cigarette carton from Jamaica and even on a poster for a Rolling

Stones European tour in 1976. Luis Trenker made a tearjerker of a film out of the tragic first ascent of the mountain (1865) by Edward Whymper, in which the four-man crew lost their lives, and in Zermatt the souvenir shops are full of Matterhorn kitsch. A mythical mountain and yet so much more than just pyramid-shaped rock?

Well, "Horu" (as it is called by locals) has brought great prosperity to the country village of Zermatt (1,616 m/5,302 ft). The hotel pioneer Alexander Seiler was the first to recognize the huge significance of this unique mountain backdrop for his tiny village. And indeed, the "mountain of mountains" has been captivating visitors since Whymper's time. They come from all over the world to marvel at this magnificent monument to Alpine altitudes, some of them even coming to climb it.

HOFBURG

COURT RIDING SCHOOL

The Hofburg was for many centuries the Habsburg monarchy's seat of political power and served as the imperial family's main residence. It also houses the present-day National Library (above, the ceremonial room), which Emperor Charles VI had built by Johann Bernhard Fischer von Erlach and his son in 1722. It was the first part of the court library.

The Spanish Riding School was not opened to the general public until after World War I. It is one of the oldest establishments for classic dressage. The performances of the legendary Lipizzaner stallions – elegant, snow-white horses originally bred in Spain – were one of the highlights of court entertainment from the 16th century.

The Hofburg, radiant in the evening light, still bears witness to the opulence with which the emperors of the Habsburg dynasty adorned their capital until the end of the monarchy in 1918.

MUSEUM OF ART HISTORY AND NATURAL HISTORY

The "twin museums" on the Burgring were designed in the early 1870s by Hamburg-born architect Gottfried Semper and Vienna native Carl von Hasenauer. The buildings look identical from the outside, but their content could hardly be more different: while the thirty-nine rooms of the Museum of Natural History (top right, a dinosaur skeleton) are home to great collections of minerals, meteorites, fossils, and skeletons as well as present-day plant and animal species, the Museum of Art History (top left, the Dome Hall) houses one of the most valuable painting galleries in the world – from Dürer and Breughel, to Rembrandt and Rubens and Tintoretto. Added to this are the Kunstkammer, coin cabinets, antiques and the Egyptian and Oriental collections.

Hugo von Hofmannsthal called the Salzburg state capital the "heart of the heart of Europe". This city not only produced Wolfgang Amadeus Mozart, but has also inspired artists from all over the world for centuries. Hohensalzburg Fortress, its Cathedral, Collegiate Church, residence, St Peter's and Mirabell Palace – the collective urban works of art on the Salzach between the hills of the Kapuzinerberg, Mönchsberg and Festungsberg dazzle the senses with their intense baroque atmosphere and fascinating range of cultural attractions. This urban gem that is the Getreidegasse (left) largely has Archbishop Wolf Dietrich von Raitenau to thank for its present-day appearance. Around 1600, the Archbishop had half of the city's medieval center demolished and the expansive central open spaces laid out. His successor, who was just as extravagantly minded, subsequently completed the unique architectural ensemble.

Hohensalzburg Fortress sits atop the Mönchsberg, below which nestles the charming Old Town.

MIRABELL

HELLBRUNN

Mirabell Palace (meaning nice view) was originally called Altenau, after Simone Alt, the mistress of Archbishop Wolf Dietrich von Raitenau, who had the palace built for his beloved in 1606. At the time its location was still outside Salzburg city limits. The palace (above, with Mirabell Garden), which was converted between 1721 and 1727 into a baroque complex by Lukas von Hildebrandt, Austria's most famous builder along with Fischer von Erlach, has been the registered office of the mayor and the magistrate since 1950.

Markus Sittikus, Count of Hohenems, the cousin and – from 1612 – successor of Archbishop Wolf Dietrich von Raitenau, built his "villa suburbana" between 1613 and 1615. It was a country pleasure palace with park complex and water features in the present-day district of Morzg. "May his successors have pleasure" is inscribed above the entrance. One of the murals in the Music Room (above), known as the "Octagon", which has ornate frescos by Donato Mascagni, depicts the Archbishop as a pink cavalier.

ROME

THE CAPITOL

FORUM ROMANUM

The center of the present-day metropolis of Rome – located at a bend in the Tiber River – was first settled around 3,000 years ago. The people who settled here left traces of their civilizations from the very start, providing Rome with tremendous appeal for anyone interested in art, architectural and cultural history.

The presence of the city's mythical founders, Romulus and Remus, can be felt during a walk through its fascinatig streets just as much as that of the other well-known Roman emperors and popes who resided in this, the capital city of Christianity, during the Renaissance and baroque periods. More than any other city, Rome is testimony to the advanced development of European culture and it is indeed here that some of the deepest roots of western civilization are to be found.

In ancient times, there was a temple on the Capitoline Hill that was dedicated to Jupiter, king of the gods. It was reached by a winding path leading south-east from the Forum. Today you climb the hill from the west on a flight of stairs designed by Michelangelo. At the top is a piazza, also designed by Michelangelo, and which is paved with a geometric pattern. The bronze equestrian sculpture of Marcus Aurelius in the center of the square (above, today a copy) is the only one of its kind to have escaped being melted down in the Middle Ages because the rider was thought to be Constantine I, defender of Christianity. The Palazzo Senatorio on the piazza is the seat of the mayor of Rome.

Located between the Palatine Hill and the Capitoline Hill, the Roman Forum and the other buildings dating from the 6th century BC were the site of religious ceremonies and political gatherings. It was here, for example, that speeches were held and all manner of merchandise offered for sale. During the day it was said to have been a bustling areal full of buyers and sellers.

The fall of the Roman Empire saw the deterioration of Forum buildings (above) such as the triumphal arch of Septimius Severus, the Temple of Saturn and the Temple of Vespasian in front of the baroque Santi Luca e Martina Church, which then fell into disuse. In the Middle Ages the Forum was known as the Campo Vaccino, the cow's meadow.

THE COLOSSEUM

Among the highlights on Capitoline Hill are the remains of a colossal statue from the 4th century BC in the courtyard of the Palace of the Conservators. It depicts Emperor Constantine I and once stood in the apse of the Basilica of Constantine on the Roman Forum. The unclothed body parts were made of marble while the rest was of bronze-clad wood.

The site where the towering ruins of the largest amphitheater in antiquity now stand was once occupied by a wooden construction that fell victim to the great fire of AD 64. Nero's included those grounds in his new palace and even had an artificial pond built. His successor Vespasian then commissioned a three-story stone arena in about the year AD 72, a magnificent building financed in part by the gold and other treasures that fell into Roman hands following the plundering of the temple in Jerusalem. The consecration of the colosseum was marked by games that lasted one hundred days during which a multitude of people and thousands of animals were killed in the name of mass entertainment.

THE PANTHEON

The Piazza della Rotonda to the west of the Via del Corso boasts one of the most impressive buildings of antiquity: the Pantheon. Built in 27 BC, the Pantheon was a temple dedicated to all of the gods, as its name implies. The round opening in the dome was of mythical significance, creating a link with the heavens. Inside the former temple are the tombs of the painter Raphael and the first king of unified Italy, Victor Emanuel II.

ST PETER'S

Facing St Peter's Square (above) is the mighty façade of St Peter's Basilica, officially known as San Pietro in Vaticano and which was built in the 16th century on the site of the apostle Peter's crucifixion. It is also where Emperor Constantine built Rome's first basilica. The present-day building is some 45 m (148 ft) high and 115 m (126 yds) wide. The height of the lantern crowning the dome is 132 m (433 ft) and the interior covers an area of 15,000 sq m (16,145 sq ft). It can accommodate around 60,000 worshippers. Naturally, the most famous artists of the age were involved in its construction: architects Bramante and Sangallo, sculptors Bernini and Maderno, and master painters Michelangelo and Raphael (both of whom were employed as architects as well). St Peter's grave is said to be located in the so-called "grotto" beneath the church.

St Peter's Basilica is an oblong building in the shape of a Latin cross. The central dome high above the crossing lets in light.

THE SISTINE CHAPEL

The Sistine Chapel, commissioned in 1477 by Pope Sixtus IV, was not just a place of worship but also a fortress with walls that are 3 m (10 ft) thick. It also continues to serve as the venue for the papal conclave, in which the College of Cardinals elects a new pope. Upon the completion of construction work in 1480, Lorenzo de' Medici, the "ruler" of Florence, sent a number of his city's leading artists to Rome to decorate the interior of the chapel with frescoes. Having waged war against the pope in the preceding years, he now wanted to make a gesture of peace. The artists included Pietro Perugino, Sandro Botticelli and Domenico Ghirlandaio. The walls were decorated with scenes from the lives of Jesus and Moses, while the ceiling of the dome was transformed into a luminescent blue sky with golden stars. It was only later, from 1508 to 1512, that it was painted over by Michelangelo.

SAN GIORGIO MAGGIORE

Benedictine monks lived San Giorgio Maggiore Island as early as the 10th century. The relics of St Stephanus of Constantinople are said to have been brought here in 1109, the result being that the church and monastery adjacent to the grave of the apostle Mark subsequently became an important pilgrimage site in the lagoon city. In 1223, the monastery was destroyed by an earthquake, but its buildings were rebuilt between the 15th and 17th centuries and those are what you see today. The Benedictine Church was designed by Andrea Palladio in 1565, its white façade having been designed to be seen from afar and its ground plan being in the shape of a Latin cross. The monks' choir and campanile were built after Palladio's death and the high altar was created by Girolamo Campagna. Two large paintings in the side aisles depict the Miracle of Manna and The Last Supper, among the last of Tintoretto's works.

ST MARK'S CATHEDRAL

Construction on St Marks Cathedral began in the 11th century on the site of two previous buildings. In allusion to the Church of the Holy Apostles in Constantinople, its ground plan is in the form of a Greek cross. The intersection and each of the arms feature vaulted domes. The cathedral's oriental aspect derives from a second construction phase that followed the Byzantine conquest. The church took on a Gothic element between the 14th and 16th centuries and the façade, situated in front of a porch, is divided into five arched portals

crowned with Byzantine-style mosaics and incorporating the treasure from Venetian raids. Above the portals is a gallery with gilded horse sculptures that the Venetians looted from Constantinople in 1204. The history of the cathedral is inextricably linked to the legend of St Mark, according to which the evangelist's remains were once miraculously transported from Alexandria to Venice where they are said to be kept to this day – in a sarcophagus far below the high altar.

THE DOGE'S PALACE

Starting in 9th century, the Doge's Palace was the residence of the Venetian head of state and the seat of the Venetian government. The present day appearance of this marble and stone masterpiece dates from the 14th and 15th centuries.

From the Piazzetta the view over the Canale di San Marco takes in the luminescent, white marble façade of the San Giorgio Maggiore church on the small island of the same name (main picture).

THE CANAL GRANDE, THE RIALTO BRIDGE

The Canale Grande is roughly 4 km (2 mi) long and lined with magnificent palaces built and owned by nearly five centuries, of merchants and nobility. It is the main traffic artery in Venice upon which a throng of gondolas and vaporetti ply their way. The end of the canal is marked on the right bank by the baroque Santa Maria della Salute Church with its wonderful dome. The roofed Rialto Bridge (above) spans the canal at about its halfway point. Originally a wooden bridge, between 1588 and 1592 it was built of stone with its present design, including two rows of shops.

POMPEII

When the crater of Mt Vesuvius exploded after centuries of tranquillity, hot magma rolled into the valley and covered Pompeii in lava and ash. A surprising number of wall paintings were preserved under the volcanic ash, as is the case with this depiction of two gods (main picture).

Vesuvius erupted on August 24 of the year AD 79, completely covering the Roman town of Pompeii under a layer of ash within roughly six hours. The neighboring town of Herculaneum was also smothered under glowing lava. After the eruption, the towns were not rebuilt and eventually forgotten. However, Pliny the Younger (ca. AD 61–113), whose uncle and adopted father were killed by the eruption, had described the event, which led the archaeologists in the right direction. The first excavations began in 1748, and today they provide an invaluable impression of life in antiquity. The remains of shops and the painted walls of splendid villas were still left standing; even petrified bread was found in the bakeries. Other discoveries included a mill, a latrine and some "graffiti" on the walls. The stepping stones that enabled passersby to cross the street without getting their feet are even still visible. The dead people are the most impressive, however, their bodies forming hollows of volcanic ash. Filled with plaster, the human figures are now visible again as silent witnesses of the eruption.

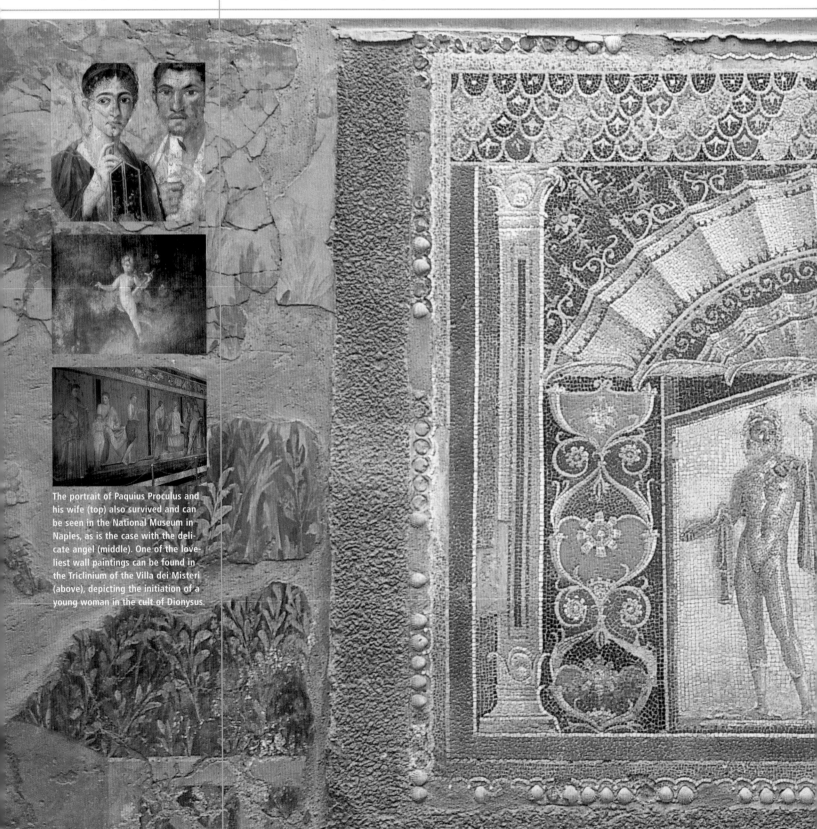

The portrait of Paquius Proculus and his wife (top) also survived and can be seen in the National Museum in Naples, as is the case with the delicate angel (middle). One of the loveliest wall paintings can be found in the Triclinium of the Villa dei Misteri (above), depicting the initiation of a young woman in the cult of Dionysus.

Around 15 km (9 mi) outside of Naples, Mt Vesuvius (left) is mainland Europe's only active volcano. Since the 18th century, excavations beneath the volcano's crater have been revealing remains of settlement in the lava layer, which is up to 7 m (23 ft) deep in places.

Excavations in Pompeii began in 1748, and since then entire streets including the buildings and the Forum (above) have been exposed. Today archeologists are primarily focused on preventing the deterioration of the ruins.

PALERMO

Palermo was the main base for the Carthaginian fleet in the First Punic War and went on to enjoy exceptional periods of cultural prosperity under the Moors, Normans and the Hohenstaufens of Germany. Thankfully, a tremendous number of historic buildings have survived from all of these epochs. In the Old Town, Byzantine churches stand next to Moorish mosques and baroque and Catalan palaces are juxtaposed with classical barracks and Arabian-style pleasure palaces. Highlights here include the splendid cathedral (above right); the Norman Palace with the mosaic-embellished Cappella Palatina (main picture), and the 16th-century Piazza Pretoria with the mannerism-style Fontana Pretoria (below). The San Cataldo, La Martorana (right) and San Giovanni degli Eremiti churches, the La Zisa Palace, the Teatro Massimo, the

catacombs of the Capuchin monastery, and the National Gallery and the Archaeological Museum are all worth seeing as well.

The lively Vucciria market (above left) on the Piazza Caracciolo is nicknamed the "belly of Palermo". It is the town's best-known market and one of the oldest in Europe. The kiosks and shops selling fish, meat, fruits and vegetables are all strung together like an oriental souk along the narrow alleyways.

MONREALE

Situated around 8 km (5 mi) from Palermo is the small episcopal town of Monreale. Monte Caputo provides fabulous views of the Sicilian capital with its bay that looks like it was drawn with a compass, the Conca d'Oro. The main sightseeing attraction here, however, is the world-famous cathedral. William II, King of Sicily, was the original benefactor of a Benedictine abbey that was built on these lofty heights in 1172, which sooned formed into a town. Seeing the growth, he had a cathedral built at its center – a basilica intended to symbolize the triumph of the Christians over the Moors. With a length of 102 m (112 ft) and a width of 40 m 140 ft, Sicily's largest church is supported by eighteen antique columns. It houses the sarcophaguses of Kings William I and II and has a magnificent bronze portal and marble floors. The mosaics (above) in the cathedral cover 6,300 sq m (67,788 sq ft) and depict stories from the Bible in incomparable splendor. The cloister – the only surviving section of the monastery – is also worth seeing with its many differently designed column pairs.

The Cappella Palatina in the Palazzo Reale (Norman Palace) was added to the palace complex between 1132 and 1240 as Roger II's court chapel. Rather modest in its outward appearance, the interior is overwhelming with its marble pillars and luminescent mosaics on a golden background. All of this is crowned with a richly decorated wooden stalactite ceiling featuring Arab ornamentation and picture stories (main picture).

GDANSK

Gdansk has a history going back more than 1,000 years, when it maintained close trade relations with Flanders, Russia and Byzantium continuing into the 12th and 13th centuries. Gdansk was a member of the Hanseatic League from 1361 and was assigned to the Polish crown in 1466. With ninety-five percent of the city in ruins at the end of World War II, Gdansk has since become a model of reconstruction work.

The most important attractions are naturally in the city center. St Mary's Church, for example, is the largest medieval brick church in Europe, its most striking feature being the 82-m-high (269-ft) bell tower. The city's Old Town comprises Long Street and the streets

adjoining it. Influential patricians built magnificent palaces like the 17th-century Hans von Eden House for themselves in the heart of the Old Town. The 15th-century Arthur's Court is among the finest examples of late-Gothic architecture in Northern Europe; the town hall, the Golden House and the Torture House are also worth seeing. One city gate from the Middle Ages has been converted into a port crane. In the northern part of the Old Town there is a series of churches, the Old Town Hall, the Small and the Large Mill and the Old Castle, which are worth visiting. The Vistula Spit, on the delta, is south of Gdansk. You can reach Malbork by crossing the spit to the south-east.

TORUN

The knights of the Teutonic Order once built a castle here, at the foot of which a town developed that went on to become a thriving commercial center in the 14th century. It even maintained its own merchant fleet for the purposes of trading with the Netherlands. The First and the Second Peace of Torun were concluded here in 1411 and 1466 between the Teu-

tonic Order and Poland. In 1454 the Teutonic Order castle was burnt down by the citizens of Torun (only remnants survive to this day) and the town became an independent city-state under the sovereignty of the Polish king. The town continued to change in appearance over the centuries, as is evidenced by the Gothic patricians' houses, the baroque and classic town houses and the opulent palaces of the 19th century. Construction of the Old Town Hall was begun in 1259, and Copernicus's birthplace dating from the 15th century has remained intact. The Cathedral of St John the Evangelist and John the Baptist as well as St Mary's Church (above left) are also worth seeing.

FROMBORK

The small town of Frombork in Warmia is culturally the most interesting town in the region with its historic complex on the cathedral hill (above). The museum next to the cathedral is dedicated to the important work of astronomist Nicholas Copernicus, who studied here. The water tower provides lovely views of the Vistula Lagoon and the port.

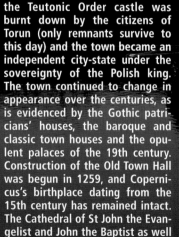

MALBORK

A white cloak with a black cross was the uniform of the Teutonic Knights, an order of knights that formed in the Holy Land during the Third Crusade (1189–1192). The knights then turned their attention to Europe just a few decades later and Prussia, along with Livonia and Courland, were subordinated and Christianized in the name of the black cross. Given sovereign powers as landlords by the emperor, the order founded towns, built castles, brought in German farmers as colonists, and promoted the arts and science. At the head of the order was the Grand Master, who was elected for life and whose seat and main fortress after 1309 was here in

Malbork Castle (main picture) on the Nogat River. It was here that all of the threads of the order's states came together, its territories already extending far into the Baltic States as well as into southern and central Germany.

The missionary work had long since become a minor priority by the time their secular rule began to crumble. The costly Battle of Tannenberg in 1410 against the more superior Poles and Lithuanians is seen to represent their beginning of the end. Held with some effort until 1457, Malbork Castle finally fell into Polish hands in 1466 with the Peace of Torun. The story of the holy state came to a definitive end in 1525 when

it became the secular Duchy of Prussia with Albrecht von Brandenburg-Ansbach as its first duke. This then became a hereditary duchy under Polish sovereignty during the Reformation.

Malbork Castle served as a barracks and a granary during the 18th century, and fell into visible disrepair during that time. The castle underwent thorough restoration in the 19th century and following the destruction of World War II it was rebuilt during the 1960s and 1970s based on original drawings.

Today the halls, chapels, corridors and courtyards house extensive museums with valuable medieval treasures.

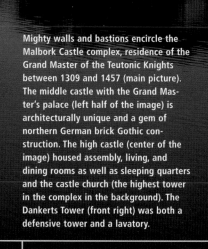

Mighty walls and bastions encircle the Malbork Castle complex, residence of the Grand Master of the Teutonic Knights between 1309 and 1457 (main picture). The middle castle with the Grand Master's palace (left half of the image) is architecturally unique and a gem of northern German brick Gothic construction. The high castle (center of the image) housed assembly, living, and dining rooms as well as sleeping quarters and the castle church (the highest tower in the complex in the background). The Dankerts Tower (front right) was both a defensive tower and a lavatory.

Early morning in the Masurian Lake District. This idyllic landscape of eastern Poland is also referred to as the "Land of a Thousand Lakes."

THE MASURIAN LAKE DISTRICT

The Masurian Lake District is a refuge for more than 350 bird species including Steppe Eagles, Mute Swans and the Common Merganser (from top).

There is no denying the magic of this landscape. Hikers, cyclists and canoeists alike can all enjoy the thoroughly fascinating water landscape here. More than 3,000 lakes are linked via rivers and canals, all mingling with wonderful forests. Gnarled trees shade cobblestone alleys that are still traveled by horse-drawn carts, while storks build their nests in the tops of the steeple. A visit to Masuria is like taking a journey back in time to the early 20th century.

Olsztyn is the main center of the Masuria region as well as the perfect starting point for excursions to a number of different sightseeing attractions, including Lidzbark Warminskj with its mighty castle that used to be the seat of the Warmia bishops. Reszel Castle nearby dates back to the 13th century.

The powerful Teutonic Knights built a castle in Kętrzyn in 1329. Beyond Kętrzyn there is a sign pointing to the north-east indicating the "Wolfsschanze" (Wolf's Lair), which Hitler built in 1939, as his headquarters. The pilgrimage church of Święta Lipka is a baroque gem.

Top to bottom: The collegiate church in Dobre Miasto north of Olsztyn; the pilgrimage church Święta Lipka; and a panje horse cart.

BIAŁOWIEŻA

Despite the extreme temperatures here, which often sink well below the freezing point in winter, this cross-border national park possesses an astounding level of biodiversity. There are some 3,000 types of mushrooms and more than a dozen species of orchids. The heavily protected central zone of the park is home to the highest trees in all of Europe: 55-m-high (180-ft) spruces and 40-m-high (131-ft) ash trees. The Polish government began using zoo animals to breed European bison (left, also known as wisents) in the 1920s, with a scheduled program of reintroducing them to the wild as of 1952. Hunting had made these primeval oxen almost extinct by the end of the 19th century, but today there are around 300 of them wandering the vast forest areas again. They are the largest species of big game in Europe.

The wild horses that used to be found throughout Eurasia and which no longer exist in the wild have also found a refuge in this protected area. In addition to rare mammals such as bears, moose, lynxes and wolves, the area is also home to more than 220 different bird species.

KRAKOW

THE MARKET SQUARE, JEWISH QUARTER

The 13th-century textile halls stand in the center of the Rynek, Krakow's market square (main picture). The ensemble originally comprised just a double row of small cloth merchants' shops, which were then amalgamated into a hall in the 14th century.

Krakow was the capital of the Polish kings until 1596, and their coronation venue from the 11th to the 18th centuries. Wawel Hill with its royal castle and cathedral remains testimony to this bygone era. The Old Town here was designed by master builders and artists from throughout Europe from the 12th to the 17th centuries. The market square, one of Europe's largest medieval town squares, is the site of the textile halls and the Gothic St Mary's Church, converted in the 14th century. The famous high altar by Veit Stoss, who created his most important works in Krakow between 1477 and 1496, can be found here. Pivotal medieval intellectuals taught at the university, founded in the 14th century. A number of Gothic, Renaissance and baroque buildings including many churches and monasteries testifying to the city's rich history. The Kazimierz Quarter was once home to a thriving Jewish community where the Old Synagogue is worthy of special mention.

St Mary's Church opposite the main market square has an especially impressive interior with magnificent wall paintings and stained glass windows (far left). Corpus Christi Church in the former Jewish Quarter of Kazimierz (left) is one of the loveliest churches in Krakow.

The Charles Bridge is 500 m (547 ft) long and its sixteen arches are supported by fifteen pillars.

VYŠEHRAD HILL

Vyšehrad Hill with St Veit's Cathedral towers over Prague. It is a castle complex that has been the country's political, intellectual and cultural center for more than 1,000 years. Formerly the royal residence, it is now the official residence of the Czech president. Access to the complex is via the first of the inner wards (above).

ST VEIT'S CATHEDRAL

Emperor Charles IV commissioned St Veit's Cathedral on the grounds of Prague Castle in 1344, as Prague was being made into an archbishopric. The nave and the choir are supported by twenty-eight pillars. The largest church in the Czech Republic, it is the burial place of emperors and kings as well as the repository for the crown jewels.

THE GOLDEN ALLEY

Franz Kafka lived for a number of years in one of these cottages in Golden Alley on the castle grounds. The cottages were built along the castle walls in the 16th century to provide lodging for watchmen and tradesmen. The assertion that alchemists were at work here under Rudolf II has not been historically proven.

The unique beauty of the historic buildings in the "Golden City", combined with centuries as a European intellectual and cultural capital have made Prague a truly wonderful place to visit. Despite having been spared much of the reckless destruction of World War II, the ravages of time have nevertheless left a definite mark on the city. Thankfully, however, competent renovations have seen this more than 1,000-year-old city on the banks of the Vltava River restored to its former glory. Indeed, the Czechs have every reason to be proud of their lovely capital city, which was formerly a grand residence of the Bohemian kings and seat of the Habsburg emperors. Their former place of residence, Vyšehrad, also provides the best views of this marvel of historical urban development.

CHARLES BRIDGE

Construction on the grand Charles Bridge began in 1357. It was later embellished with its masterful baroque statues between 1707 and 1714. the bridge takes you from the Lesser Quarter, the area beneath Vyšehrad Hill, over the Vltava River to the Old Town. Its decor is based on the baroque figures of the saints on the Ponte Sant'Angelo in Rome, the most famous of which is the bronze statue of St John of Nepomuk from 1683. It honors the preacher and saint, John Nepomuk, whom King Wenceslas IV had thrown from the bridge into the Vltava River at this spot. The bridge is named after King Charles IV (1316–1378).

LESSER QUARTER

1756. The Lesser Quarter was initially inhabited mainly by artisans because the rents were very low. It was only in the 17th century that this area of the city enjoyed an upswing, with new churches, monasteries and 200 aristocrats' palaces being built here under Hapsburg rule.

Prague's Lesser Quarter, which was legally an independent town from 1257 to 1784, is reached via the Lesser Quarter gate on the Charles Bridge. This area beneath the Prague Castle is dominated by the baroque St Nicholas Church with its 75-m-high (246-ft) dome that was built between 1702 and

BUDAPEST

BUDA, ÓBUDA, PEST

Buda, Óbuda (Old Buda) and Pest were all joined in 1872 to form "BudaPest," the new capital of the former Kingdom of Hungary. The royal castle town of Buda has largely retained its medieval character, with numerous Gothic and baroque buildings lining the narrow streets. Trinity Square lies at the center of the castle hill, which has been a municipality since the 17th century, and is dominated by the Church of Our Lady. Originally built in 1250, the church underwent a neo-Gothic conversion in the 19th century. Its south portal now features a tympanum relief comprised of original pieces from the high-Gothic building.

The royal castle, built on the site of a structure that was destroyed in the great siege of 1686, was begun in 1749 and is located just to the south of the castle hill. The excavation sites of the Roman settlement of Aquincum, with its large amphitheater that accommodated some 13,000 spectators, can be found in Óbuda. The monumental, classical-style synagogue was erected in 1820 and is also worth visiting.

Pest is situated on the other side of the Danube. This commercial town was a center of middle-class and intellectual life in the 19th century. The buildings around the city ring are especially impressive.

PARLIAMENT

The parliament building with its magnificent staircase is based on its counterpart in London and was built between 1885 and 1904 according to plans by Imre Steindl.

ST MATTHEW'S CHURCH

Construction of St Matthew's (below and inset right) took place between 1255 and 1269 and was commissioned by King Béla IV. King Louis the Great converted it into a Gothic hall church with a nave and two side aisles at the turn of the 15th century. King Matthias Corvinus then expanded the church with a five-floor tower and the royal oratorio in 1470.

THE GELLÉRT BATHS

Built in the Secessionist (Art Nouveau) style and opened in 1918, the Gellért Hotel and the Gellért Baths are the most famous in Budapest. The men's baths, the outdoor pools, and the thermal and steam baths for women are opulent in their design and decorated with lovely mosaics. Above the baths on the hill is a monument commemorating the baths' namesake, the martyred Bishop Gellért who, according to legend, was rolled into the Danube in a sealed barrel at this site.

FISHERMEN'S BASTION

The Fishermen's Bastion was built between 1895 and 1902 on the site of the old fish market in Buda. The architect Frigyes Schulek, who was also responsible for the neo-Gothic conversion of St Matthew's Church, based the building's conical towers on the tents of the Magyar people.

THE CHAIN BRIDGE

ST STEPHEN'S, OPERA HOUSE

The oldest of the nine bridges in Budapest is the Chain Bridge. Preparations for the first piers began on July 28, 1840, with wooden pickets first being driven into the bank to cordon off the construction site. The neoclassical construction is still supported by two triumphal arch-like buttresses that contain the iron chains of the bridge body, which measures a total of 375 m (1,237 ft).

The impressive dimensions of this magnificent church, which can accommodate around 8,500 people, become apparent with a glance at the almost 100-m-high (328-ft) dome with its wonderful mosaic decoration. The Hungarian state opera is a popular venue for extravagant musical productions (above).

Today there are nine bridges linking the districts of Buda (with Old Buda) and Pest (main picture; the Elizabeth Bridge in the foreground, with the Chain Bridge directly behind it).

THE PLITVICE LAKES

The sixteen lakes of Plitvice Lakes National Park, close to the border with Bosnia-Herzegovina, are connected by terraces, cascades and waterfalls and are testimony to the constantly changing yet pristine natural panorama of Croatian limestone. The chain of lakes extends over about 7 km (4 mi) and owes its existence to calcification and sinkholes.

Over several thousand years the limestone sinter has formed barriers and dams behind which the water pools up; algae and mosses are the reason for the shimmering blue and green hues of the twelve larger lakes.

The most impressive waterfalls, with drops of up to 76 m (249 ft), are near the four lower lakes. The lime-enriched water plunges over numerous terraces, themselves constantly collapsing and reforming, into the tiny ponds (left and main picture). The Korana is the end of the lakes where the Plitvica flows out.

The region at the foot of the mountain range known as the Small Kapela was declared a national park in 1949 and boasts rich flora and fauna. The dense forests are home to about 120 bird species as well as to deer, wolves and brown bears.

Dubrovnik was one of the most important centers of trade with the Eastern Mediterranean (the Levant) during the Middle Ages. Known at the time as Ragusa – Dubrovnik being its official name only since 1919 –, the town successfully fended off claims to power in the 14th century by the Venetians and the Hungarians. Officially under Turkish rule as of 1525, it determined its own fate as a free republic up until the annexation of Dalmatia by Napoleon in 1809. Its mighty fortresses, with walls up to 6 m (20 ft) thick and 25 m (82 ft) high remain a testimony to its strength.

Ragusa was a bastion of Humanism in its time and had a tremendous influence on Slavic literature and painting. It was here that Croatian developed as a literary language between the 15th and 17th centuries. The town was almost entirely destroyed by an earthquake in 1667, but the large medieval buildings like the Rector's Palace and the monastery have been renovated. Most of the structure, some of the interior decor, and the imposing cathedral were rebuilt in the baroque style.

One of the highlights of a trip to Romania is an excursion through the Danube Delta. This mighty river divides into three main arms close to Tulcea, more than 2,800 km (1,740 mi) from its source in Germany and almost 80 km (50 mi) before its estuary on the Black Sea coast. The three broad waterways encompass a wetland of around 4,500 sq km (1,737 sq mi), a unique ecosystem that is home to the world's largest cohesive reed cluster (over 800 sq km/309 sq mi). This vast network of waterways, backwaters, canals, lakes, islands, floodplain forests and marshes is also home to a huge diversity of animals and plants. The mighty gallery forests of oaks, willows and poplars are overgrown with lianas and creepers, an especially impressive sight. Water lilies and floating reed islands (Plaurs) cover vast expanses of the water. The diversity of the bird life is also particularly striking, with huge flocks of pelicans and cormorants, for example, and fish eagles and egrets – so rare elsewhere.

Gliding slowly through the narrow channels in a boat or crossing one of the lakes is a wonderful experience in this seemingly forgotten natural paradise. Only seldom do you get a glimpse of the reed-covered huts, which serve as seasonal homes for the fishermen, beekeepers and reed cutters. A fishing village will occasionally crop up, typically inhabited by Romanians as well as Ukrainians and Lipovans, the descendants of 17th-century Russian immigrants. The impression of a fully intact wilderness is deceptive, however. Now protected as a biosphere reserve, the natural equilibrium of the delta also suffered massive disruption, particularly in the 1980s, as a result of haphazard tree felling, irresponsible drainage practices, hunting and livestock farming.

The floodplain forest along the Danube estuary on the Black Sea coast is flooded in the spring (main picture); water chestnuts cover large areas of its surface (right).

The bird life of the Danube Delta
includes members of the egret family
such as the Squacco Heron (right,
a courting display). This is also the
main breeding ground for the endangered White Pelican (far right).

ACROPOLIS

Settlement on the fortress hill in Athens can be traced back to the New Stone Age. The former royal fort was converted into a religious site as far back as the 6th century BC. After being destroyed by the Persians, the sanctuaries were quickly rebuilt in the second half of the 5th century BC. The image of Athens' Acropolis is now dominated by the Parthenon.

This temple, built between 447 and 422 BC, was dedicated to the goddess of the city, Pallas Athene. The structure is flanked by a series of mighty columns with eight across the ends and seventeen along the sides. The cult image of Athena once adorned the interior of the temple, the so-called Cella. The inside and outside of the building were decorated with elaborate, three-dimensional marble statues, of which only part still exist today. The gable reliefs in the west, for example, depict Athena's birth, while those in the east illustrate her epic battle with Poseidon.

The Erechtheion, named after the mythical king of Athens, was built between 421 and 406 BC. It is home to several cult sites,

which explains the unusual layout of the complex. The structure is surrounded by three large porches; the roof of the Caryatid Porch is supported by columns in the shape of young women (left and below). The Propylaea are the monumental gate complexes of the walls surrounding the Acropolis. They are considered the masterpiece of architect Mnesikles and were built between 437 and 432 BC. The variety of column arrangements here are remarkable. While the entire façade is Doric, the slender Ionic columns rise up in the central passage. Kallikrates' temple of Athena Nike was built between 425 and 421 BC, and is one of the oldest remaining buildings in Ionic style. The small but elegant temple has porches on both the eastern and western side.

Athens is the capital of Greece and a fast-paced international metropolis of five million people overlooking the Aegean. The sea of white houses is surrounded on three sides by mountains up to 1,413 m (4,636 ft) and scattered with bare cliffs poking up like islands. One of these rises bears the heart of ancient European culture, the Acropolis. At its feet, modern life pulsates, stretching as far as Piraeus, the port city on the Saronic Gulf.

PLÁKA UND PSIRRÍ

Athens' most beautiful historic quarter is the Pláka, right below the Acropolis. You'll find eateries, small hotels and of course a slew of souvenir stores here among the stately neoclassical villas from the 19th century. Folklore is the focus in the music taverns of the steep "Odós Mnisikléous" alleyway. Hollywood stars act on the screen of the "Cine Paris" rooftop garden cinema, flanked by the illuminated backdrop of the Acropolis, while priests purchase their liturgical accesories and robes at Athens' Orthodox cathedral. The adjacent merchant and handicrafts quarter, Psirrí, has become the hip place to be, but many artisans and merchants still pursue their trade here during the day.

DIMOTIKÍ AGORÁ

The "Dimotikí Agorá" market is over 100 years old and still the best address for fresh meat and fish. Although the products are now displayed in glass freezers and include everything from hen and sheep tongues to cow hearts and lamb cutlets, they are always artistically organized on their various shelves. The market halls are also a popular meeting place for both night owls and early risers – the market's taverns are open around the clock. Cheese, nut and olive dealers have their stalls outside while fruit, vegetable, sausages and stockfish are traded on the opposite side of the road.

View of the Acropolis from the south, with the mighty Parthenon in the center of the complex. Lykabettos Hill is in the background on the right.

The Poseidon Temple, built on Cape Soúnio between 444 and 440 BC, is visible from great distances rising up at the southern tip of the Attic Peninsula.

DELPHI

From the 8th century BC, Delphi was one of the most important sanctuaries of ancient times. In the center of the holy district was a temple for Apollo (below)

where Pythia, a divine priestess, presided over the famous Oracle of Delphi. The Pythic Games were held every four years, with the musical and literary competitions held in the now well-preserved theater, and the athletic disciplines were held in the stadium, located at the highest part of the sanctuary perched above the Corinthian Gulf. A large monastery was built east of Delphi in the 10th century. Its church is one of three places of worship in Greece whose magnificent mosaic decorations were largely preserved from the time around the year 1100.

OLYMPIA

An ancient document registers the name of the first winner of a track race in the Sanctuary of Zeus in Olympia in the year 776 BC, a date that has since been considered the date of the first Olympic Games. They were held every four years for over 1,350 years until a Byzantine emperor

forbade them as heathen practices. Near the village of Olimbía, German archaeologists have been excavating the stately remains of this ancient cult district, including its sporting sites, for more than 100 years; the Olympic flame for the modern Olympic Games is always lit here at the Temple of Hera. Three museums display masterpieces of ancient art and sporting aspects of the Olympic Games in both ancient and modern times. The Nike of Paionios (top) is one of the things to be admired there.

EPIDAUROS

The complex of Epidauros, located in a narrow valley in the far eastern reaches of the Peloponnese, spans several levels. It is of key importance to the Asklepios cult, which spread throughout all of Greece in the 5th century BC. In Greek mythology, the god of medicine was the son of Apollo, whose powers of healing were also channeled through him.

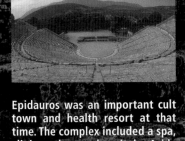

Epidauros was an important cult town and health resort at that time. The complex included a spa, clinic and even hospitals. Aside from the Temple of Asklepios, the most important monuments are the Temple of Artemis, the Tholos, the Enkoimeterion, and the Propylaea. The most impressive example of classic Greek architecture in Epidauros is the theater (above), dating back to the early 3rd century BC. It is the best preserved building of its kind in Greece, and is particularly remarkable because of its excellent acoustics.

MYCENAE

The Mycenaean culture, which dominated the entire eastern Mediterranean from the 15th to the 12th centuries BC, played an invaluable role in the development of classical Greece. Its name was taken from the Bronze Age fort, Mycenae, in the eastern Peloponnese. The region had already been settled since

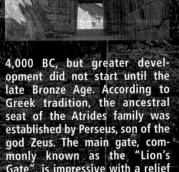

4,000 BC, but greater development did not start until the late Bronze Age. According to Greek tradition, the ancestral seat of the Atrides family was established by Perseus, son of the god Zeus. The main gate, commonly known as the "Lion's Gate", is impressive with a relief of two mighty – but now headless – lions (top). Just behind that is the royal graves district where German archaeologist Heinrich Schliemann found the gold funeral mask of Agamemnon, who led the Greeks against Troy.

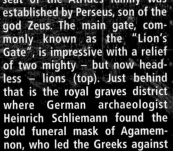

SOÚNIO

The Temple of Poseidon in Soúnio, whose sixteen remaining Doric marble columns still support the epistyle on which the temple's roof once rested. The location marks the southern border of Attika, which starts in the north near Egósthena at the Corinthian Gulf and Skála Oropoú at the Southern Euboean Gulf. In ancient times, Attika was basically the bread basket of Athens' agricultural hinterland. Slaves originally laid the foundations for Athens' wealth in the silver mines of Lávrio near Soúnio. In the Demeter Sanctuary of the present-day industrial city of Elefsína, free citizens wanted to demand better conditions for the afterlife by participating in this mysterious cult. In ancient times, the crews of Athenian war and trading ships thanked the temperamental god of the sea for their safe return at the Temple of Poseidon, partly decorated in gaudy colors. People hoped to be healed of illnesses in the Amphiáreion, while pregnant women made pilgrimages to Brauron to ask for assistance from the Goddess Artemis.

GOLDEN HORN, GALATA BRIDGE, YENI CAMI MOSQUE

This city with three names – Byzantium, Constantinople and Istanbul – has experienced two empires in its history that significantly shaped the success of the Mediterranean for almost 2,000 years: the East Roman, or Byzantine, Empire and its direct successor, the Ottoman Empire. According to legend, the Byzantines fleeing the Ottomans threw so many treasures into the port basin that the water glistened gold. The "Golden Horn" (main picture with the Galata Bridge and the Yeni Cami Mosque, completed in 1663) was born. Istanbul has a unique relationship with the sea. The waters flow from the Black Sea through the Bosporus Strait, into the Sea of Marmara and the Dardanelles and out into the Aegean Sea. Indeed, a sought-after piece of real estate.

BLUE MOSQUE

The foundations of the Sultan Ahmed or "Blue" Mosque were laid in 1609, and the massive project was completed relatively quickly by 1616. Sultan Ahmed I, its sponsor, died one year after the mosque was finished. The colossal mosque, whose interior is decorated with predominantly blue Iznik tiles – hence its name – owes its spaciousness to the 43-m-high (141-ft) dome. It rests on four striking pillars, as well as four ascending half-domes, and has a diameter of 23.5 m (77 ft). The Mihrab, the prayer room, is made of marble and adorned with precious stones.

The Golden Horn (main picture, with the Galata Bridge and the Yeni Cami mosque from 1663) is one of the world's best natural ports.

The Kremlin panorama in Moscow (main picture with the promenade along the Moskva River) is characterized by an entire ensemble of fortress and church towers. The present-day design of Russia's center of power dates from its reconstruction after Napoleon destroyed it in 1812.

THE KREMLIN

Russia's capital lies on the Moskva River, a tributary of the Volga. First mention was made of it in 1147, and by 1325 it had become a grand ducal residence. During the reign of Czar Peter the Great, Moscow lost its capital city status in 1713 to newly founded St Petersburg. It was the Bolsheviks who made Moscow the political center of Russia again in 1918. Over the course of its history the city has been plundered repeatedly as well as suffering devastating fires. At the beginning of the 20th century Moscow boasted 450 churches, twenty-five monasteries, and 800 charitable institutions. After the disintegration of the USSR, the metropolis (with more than 10 million residents) still has an impressive cultural complement. With over sixty theaters, seventy-five museums, 100 colleges and about 2,300 historic buildings, Moscow maintains a leading position among the world's cities.

For centuries, historical and political events in Russia have been inextricably linked to the Moscow Kremlin, seat of the czars and the metropolitan bishops since the 13th century. Architecturally speaking, the Kremlin had already attained its current size at the time of Grand Prince Ivan IV, known as Ivan the Terrible, who had himself crowned as czar in 1547. First mention of the city's defensive wall was documented in 1147; it was still a wooden construction until the 14th century. Ivan the Terrible gradually had the city walls and the numerous churches almost entirely rebuilt by the leading Italian and Russian master builders of the time, preferring instead to have more ostentatious buildings constructed in their place. These grand edifices were continuously expanded and remodeled until well into the 20th century. They now house priceless works of art. The Kremlin is still Russia's seat of government, for which the term "Kremlin" is synonymous. Within its walls are magnificent palaces, armories, senate buildings, as well as cathedrals and churches with characteristic gilded domes. The Church of the Deposition (Zerkov Rispoloscheniya) was constructed by Russian builders in 1485 and is the seat of the Russian patriarchs and metropolitan bishops. The name derives from a Byzantine feast day celebrating the arrival of the Mother of God's robes in Constantinople. The valuable interior decor includes a 17th-century icon wall (above left).

RED SQUARE, ST BASIL'S CATHEDRAL

Red Square (below) is roughly 500 x 150 m (1,640 x 492 ft) and was built at the end of the 15th century as a market and gathering place, in addition to its use as a place of execution. The famous St Basil's Cathedral (right) was built by Ivan the Terrible after his victory over the Mongol Golden Horde. The cathedral, consecrated in 1561, is considered an outstanding masterpiece of Old Russian construction. The central, steepled church is surrounded by eight chapels on a single foundation and arranged in the shape of a cross. It was the addition of the St Basil's Chapel that gave the whole complex its name. The central building with the pavilion roof is dominated by the nine differently designed chapels.

GUM

At the time of its completion in 1893, GUM, which was designed as a marketplace and today one of the largest department stores in the world, was considered one of the most advanced buildings in Russia with its steel and glass roof. Architect Pomeranzev combined both Renaissance and traditional Russian architectural elements in the building, designing it as a shopping center with the shops strung together.

After Czar Peter the Great had forced the Swedish King Karl XII to part with a strip of coastline along the Gulf of Finland, he finally gained his long-awaited access to the Baltic Sea, and thus to the West. He then built his new capital there, St Petersburg, which was intended to outmatch the splendor of other European cities. A great number of master architects and builders from Western and Central Europe such as Bartolomeo Rastrelli, Domenico Trezzini and Andreas Schlüter were involved in the construction of St Petersburg, a city that is particularly impressive with regard to the harmony created between its baroque and classical styles, grandiose squares, and numerous canals with more than 400 bridges. Nevsky Prospekt, St Petersburg's magnificent promenade, is lined with ostentatious buildings such as the Anitchkov and Stroganov Palaces.

THE WINTER PALACE

The Winter Palace (main picture and above: the splendid Jordan Staircase) is one of the most significant buildings in Russian baroque style. Begun in 1754 based on plans drawn up by Bartolomeo Rastrelli, it was intended as be an imperial residence directly alongside the Neva River. The Winter Palace is the largest component of the Hermitage complex.

THE HERMITAGE

The Hermitage is one of the most important art museums in the world. It comprises the Winter Palace, the Small, the New and the Old Hermitage, as well as the Hermitage Theater. The Hermitage art collection, which was started by Catherine the Great, is a museum of superlatives (right). The more than 1,000 magnificently designed rooms display around 60,000 exhibits, while the archive encompasses three million items. In addition to the archaeological section with exhibits dating back to antiquity, visitors can also enjoy a massive collection of classical European art.

Today the former Winter Palace (main picture, from the banks of the Neva), main residence of the czars in St Petersburg, houses one of the most famous art museums in the world.

PALACE SQUARE

The Winter Palace owes its current design to Peter the Great's successor, Empress Elizabeth. In fact, the building where the Emperor died in 1725 – on the site that is now occupied by the Hermitage Theater – was torn down completely to make way for the new palace. The square in front of the Winter Palace with the Alexander Column (right) has been the scene of key historical events. It was here that more than 1,000 demonstrators were murdered by czarist troops in 1905, and it was here that the October Revolution began in 1917, when the Bolsheviks stormed the grounds.

The world's highest mountains, vast shimmering deserts and dense misty rainforests are all hallmarks of Asia, the largest continent on earth. The cultures from the Euphrates and Tigris rivers were the cradle of human civilizations. The empires of the ancient Orient, of Islam, Hinduism, and Buddhism all generated an immeasurably rich cultural heritage. One example are the rice terraces built into steep mountain slopes on Bali (main picture), a testament to skills developed over centuries.

ALEPPO

The north-western part of what is now Syria has been a cultural hotbed for thousands of years and Aleppo, a town situated at the crossroads of ancient trading routes, possesses many well pre-served examples of this history. Excavations on Citadel Hill prove that it is in fact one of the oldest continuously inhabited places in the world – settled in the third millennium BC. Two monuments stand out in Aleppo's Old Town, which is richly endowed with medieval madrassas, palaces, car-avanserais and bath houses: the Citadel (main picture) and the Friday Mosque, built in 715 by the Omayyads and rebuilt in 1190.

Until its conversion in the year 705, the Omayyad Friday Mosque in Damascus also served as a Christian church. Colonnaded walkways decorated with Byzantine mosaics enclose the larger inner courtyard and several pavilions (main picture). Left: An arched bridge leads to the upper gatehouse of Aleppo's Citadel, built in 1211.

DAMASCUS

While the façades of the Sayyida Ruqayya Mosque, the main Shiite mosque in the Old Town of Damascus, are fairly plain, its interior decoration counts as one of the most beautiful examples of Persian interior architecture. The mosque was completed in 1985 with financial support from Iran, and houses the mausoleum of Ruqayya bint al-Hussein ash-Shaheed bi-Kerbala, a granddaughter in-law of the Prophet Mohammed and the daughter of the martyr, Hussein of Kerbala (above). The shrine is decorated with solid gold plates, and the walls are adorned with polychrome mosaics.

Mohammed himself is said to have refused to visit the city of Damascus because he did not wish to enter any paradise other than that awaiting him in Heaven. Today the city still does justice to its poetic name, "Diamond of the Desert". The cityscape has been marked by Islam since the eighth century. The Great Mosque was built on the foundations of a Christian church in 705, at the zenith of Omayyad rule. It is one of the oldest Islamic prayer houses and a trend-setter in Islamic architecture. In the immediate vicinity of the Omayyad Mosque are the city's famous markets (souks), including the roofed Souk al-Hamidiyya (below), and other treasures of Islamic architecture such as Maristan Nureddin, a hospital built in 1154; the Nureddin Madrassa; and the tomb of Saladin from the year 1193.

JERUSALEM

"People are nothing more than temporary guests on this earth, but the people of Jerusalem are temporary guests on a part of the earth that is permeated with eternity."
Schalom Ben-Chorin

THE OLD CITY

There are few other places in the world that are as intertwined with world history as Jerusalem. The city offers a multifaceted journey through time, with the great monuments of Judaism, Christianity and Islam clearly visible to all – and most are located within the Old City of Jerusalem and its fortified walls. The main sites include the Citadel with the Tower of David; the Armenian Quarter with the St James Cathedral; the Jewish Quarter with the Ha'ari and Ramban synagogues; the ruins of the Hurva Synagogue; the "Burnt House"; and the Western Wall, the most important Jewish sanctuary. Nearly one-sixth of the Old City is taken up by the Temple Mount where, according to the Old Testament, Abraham sacrificed his son Isaac. The Via Dolorosa, the "Road of Pain" along which Jesus carried his crucifix in the New Testament, leads via the fourteen Stations of the Cross up to Calvary with the Church of the Holy Sepulcher on Temple Mount. In the middle of the Temple Mount area stands the mosaic-adorned Dome of the Rock.

THE WESTERN WALL

The Western or Wailing Wall is a 48-m (130-ft) section of a wall dating back to the Second Temple. Built on the site of the Holy Temple, it is one of the most sacred sites in Judaism, a pilgrimage destination where slips of paper containing prayers, wishes and thanks can be placed into cracks in the wall.

JEWISH QUARTER

This neighborhood below the Western Wall has been settled by Jews since the eighth century BC but their presence grew through the 13th century when they began building Talmud Torah schools and synagogues. In 1701, construction of the Hurva Synagogue began under Rabbi Yehuda Hassid. When the Jewish cleric died, however, construction was halted and the synagogue was not completed until 150 years later. It was then destroyed by the Jordanians during the 1948 Arab-Israeli War. The ruins have been preserved as a memorial (above).

According to the Jewish faith, the Messiah will one day sit in the Last Judgment in the Kidron Valley below the Mount of Olives. A Jewish cemetery with a memorial was therefore built on this hill north-east of the Old Town (left).

DOME OF THE ROCK

At the end of the seventh century, during the reign of Caliph Abd al-Malik, Byzantine and Arab architects built the Dome of the Rock on the Temple Mount, the oldest of all sacred Islamic buildings. Stained-glass windows allow soft light to flood the interior of the cupola, which is supported by colonnaded arcades.

THE HOLY SEPULCHER

Six Christian denominations share the Church of the Holy Sepulcher on Temple Mount (top). It marks the location of the Resurrection of Christ (right). The Roman Catholic Chapel of the Invention of the Holy Cross is said to be on the spot where the True Cross of Christ was found (above).

The most important archeological relic of the Nabataeans is hidden in the Jebel Haroun Mountains, midway between the Gulf of Aqqaba and the Dead Sea: Petra. The "Rock city" is Petra's most famous building and was known to the Bedouins as the "Pharaoh's Treasure House".

PETRA

In 169 BC the Nabataeans chose for their capital a place that enjoyed perfect natural protection: the bottom of the Wadi Musa valley behind the narrow Siq Gorge, which is only a few meters wide but 200 m (656 ft) deep and thus virtually inaccessible to would-be invaders. The most impressive structures of Petra are giant rock graves that were hewn into the rock, their splendid façades presenting an impressive interplay of traditional Arab construction methods and Hellenic architecture featuring mighty columns, cornices and gables. Richly adorned tombs with interesting names make it apparent that the Nabataeans believed in life after death.

WADI RUM

The roughly 50-km-long (31-mi) valley is one of Jordan's most fascinating destinations (above) where for centuries Howeitat Bedouins (right) have lived with their camels and goats. Today, many of them work as guides in the desert valley and the protected nature reserve. People have made use of the favorable conditions here since prehistoric times as countless wells can be found at the dividing line between the bizarre sandstone formations and the much deeper impermeable granite plinth. Less known is the fact that the Wadi Rum is a rich source of phosphate, which is mined here and constitutes an important source of income for Jordan.

According to Islam, every Muslim should visit the Kaaba (Arabic for "cube") in Mecca at least once in his life, to shout there like Abraham and Mohammed: "Labaik Allahumma labaik!" ("Here I am, oh God, here I am!"). The Kaaba, in the courtyard of the main mosque, Masjid al-Haram, is a windowless, cube-shaped building covered by a black silk and golden curtain (kiswah) that is replaced every year. The main picture here shows a pilgrim touching the Ruknu l-Aswad or "Black Stone", on the eastern corner of the otherwise empty Kaaba. It was already venerated by Arab tribes in pre-Islamic days. According to legend, Abraham, the first of the Biblical patriarchs and progenitor of the people of Israel, received the stone from the Arch-angel Gabriel as a gift from Paradise. In fact, there are many legends relating to this stone, which has never actually been scientifically examined and is believed by some to be a meteorite. It is thus said to have originally been white – it is the grief over the sins of men, so it is said, that gradually turned the stone black (main picture).

MECCA

MEDINA

As the birthplace of the Prophet Mohammed (c. 570–632), Mecca, situated in western Saudi Arabia, is the holiest and most important sacred site in Islam. Every year millions of worshippers make the pilgrimage to the town, forbidden to non-Muslims. In the courtyard of the mosque with its seven minarets (above) is the Kaaba, a cube-shaped building that is said to date back to Abraham.

Medina is the second most important pilgrimage destination in Islam, and is also closed to non-Muslims. Mohammed and his daughter Fatima are buried in the Great Mosque (above).

SANA'A

The town of Sana'a dates back to a fortress from Sabaean days. It prospered under the rule of the Himyarite kings after 520. In 628 present-day Yemen became part of an Islamic caliphate; Mohammed himself is believed to have supervised the building of the first mosque in Sana'a. The Great Mosque from that time is certainly impressive, yet it is undisputedly the Old Town which possesses the most historic significance. Ancient "skyscrapers" that are up to 1,000 years old were built in Sana'a, some of them boasting up to eight floors. The lower floors were built in traditional style using natural stone while the upper floors were constructed using mud bricks. The look of the façades of these tower houses is especially remarkable. Decorative elements adorn the houses, which have white trim and stucco friezes that indicate the height of each floor. The most common features are the mostly semicircular skylight openings that are framed by stucco carvings with floral or geometric designs and decorated with stained glass.

SHIBAM

The impressive high-rise houses built from air-dried bricks and rammed clay are characteristic of the well-preserved historic center of the desert town of Shibam in the Hadramaut region. The Old Town and its 500 homes, some of them rising to eight or nine floors – nearly 30 m (98 ft) high – is the earliest example of vertical urban planning.

Mud-brick tower blocks with artfully decorated façades litter the Old Town of Sana'a (main picture), capital of Yemen and once among the most beautiful places on the Incense Route.

"Las Vegas on the Gulf" attracted seafarers from Great Britain and India back at the beginning of the 20th century, at a time when the trade in gold was already an important pillar of the economy. Indeed, the rulers of Dubai do not simply rely on oil when planning for the future. Aside from the Jebel Ali Free Zone and the international airport, tourism is adding increasing amounts of money to the state's coffers. Luxury hotels are built in neo-Oriental style and new beaches are created using the finest white sand. One of the most recent and most impressive examples of making seemingly utopian dreams come true are the Palm Islands (below), the new icon of Dubai locatednext to the Burj Al Arab Hotel (main picture), which is shaped like the sail of a *dhow*, and the Burj Dubai (far left), completed in 2009 – at 818 m (2,684 ft) the highest skyscraper in the world. Next to them, the old houses with their wind towers are quite modest. Divided in two by Dubai Creek (al-Khor), the emirate markets itself is as

"the most beautiful shopping paradise in the world" with lively bazaars, or *souks*, arranged in covered shopping alleys (above). In the south-west is Bur Dubai with the Dubai Museum in the old Al-Fahidi Fortress and the oldest district, Bastakiah. On the other side of the Creek, in the Deira port district, you can still get an idea of life in the Emirates before the oil boom. This is where the *dhows* anchor, merchant boats with triangular sails that were in use in pre-Islamic days.

The Burj Al Arab in Dubai, built as a
stylized sail, is the only 7-star hotel
in the world.

ISFAHAN

In the 16th and 17th centuries, Isfahan, about 350 km (217 mi) south of Tehran in the foothills of the Zagros Mountains, developed as a center of Islamic architecture and scholarship. Shah Abbas I (1587–1629) was obsessed with construction and made extensive changes to his residence. During his reign, Isfahan became one of the most important cities in the Orient as far as culture and art are concerned. His most important building project was the vast Naghsh-e Jahan Square (the "Design of the World"), later renamed Meidan-e-Shah ("Royal Square"), and since the revolution known as Meidan-e Imam (Imam Square).

Surrounded by two-story arcades and extending over a length of 500 m (1,600 ft), it is among the largest squares in the world. The square is framed in by four remarkable building complexes: the former royal mosque known as Imam Mosque on the south side; the Sheikh Lotfollah Mosque (left) on the east side; the royal Ali Qapu Palace ("High Gate", below) on the west side; and the main portal to the Royal Qeisarieh Bazaar on the north side. The most important edifice on the grand square is the Imam Mosque (main picture and opposite page) with its four tall iwans typical of Iranian-Islamic four-iwan architecture.

The four 27-m-high (89-ft) entrance portals to the Imam Mosque feature magnificent decorations. *Muqarnas*, which fill the niche above the main portal with a stalactite-type ornamentation, are one of the typical style elements (main picture). The mosque has a separate area for women (left) as well as superb tiles and mosaics.

The Achaemenid King Darius I, the most important ruler of the Achaemenid dynasty, laid the foundation stone for the royal palace of Persepolis in 520 BC. Although he already had two capitals at the time – Pasargadae and Susa – he wished to present the world with an outstanding residence that would reflect the size of his empire. The result was the most magnificent work of Achaemenidic Persian art, built on an artificial terrace covering 125,000 sq m (1,345,000 sq ft). The royal buildings took almost sixty years to complete. A relief in the treasure house of Persepolis depicts Great King Darius I receiving a delegation of Medeans who had been subjugated by a predecessor of his, Cyrus II.

Darius I himself only lived to see the completion of the palace, the treasury and the colonnaded hall (Apadana) with its thirty-six columns measuring nearly 20 m (66 ft) and featuring superb reliefs (above and main picture). It was his son Xerxes who continued with the ambitious plans. The main entrance to the royal residence (top) that he had built was known as the "Gate of all Nations". Everyone had to be registered there upon arrival in order to be considered for an audience with the king. However, the "Dream of Darius" was laid to waste as early as the year 330 BC by Alexander the Great. The last Shah of Iran, Reza Pahlavi, had some parts of the town rebuilt in 1971.

The 70-m-long (77-yd) relief on the eastern ascent of the colonnaded hall of Persepolis depicts the delegates of twenty-eight nations from the Achaemenid Empire who had come to pay tribute for the New Year. They are sporting traditional attire and hairstyles from their regions (main picture).

Northern Pakistan is dominated by enormous mountain ranges that continue into China to the east. The Karakoram, as they are called, join the Himalayas here in the Hindu Kush and boast some of the highest peaks on earth. In fact, about half of the world's one hundred highest summits are in the Karakoram, all within a very small area. The tallest peak in the range – K2, at 8,614 m (28,263 ft) – is also the second-highest on earth. The Karakoram Highway, a combined project between Pakistan and China that was completed in 1978 after about twenty years of construction, is 1,284 km (798 mi) long and connects Havelian in north-west Pakistan with Kashgar in the western Chinese province of Xinjiang. Snaking its way past 8,000-m (25,000-ft) peaks such as Nanga Parbat, the Karakoram Highway – the highest road in the world – reaches its highest point on the 4,733-m (15,529-ft) Khunjerab Pass, which also marks the border between Pakistan and China. The architectural style of the 600-year-old Baltit Fort, former residence of the commander of Hunza, also reveals Tibetan influences. In 1979, German ethnographer Karl Jettner discovered some 30,000 rock paintings and inscriptions in the Hunza and Indus valleys (below), the oldest of which are from the Early Bronze Age. Left: The Hunza Valley after a storm.

The Baltoro Glacier (main picture) is 57 km (35 mi) long and covers an area of 754 sq km (291 sq mi), making it one of the largest glaciers outside the polar regions.

Spacious halls with finely decorated vaults, columns and windows are typical of the structures of the Red Fort (main picture). The shapes and patterns combine Persian and Central Asian elements with Indian and Hindu architectural styles.

QUTB MINAR

At the end of the 12th century, Muslims under Qutb-ud-din Aybak conquered northern India and the Rajput fortress of Lal Kot, a settlement that preceded the foundation of Delhi. When they erected their first mosque there, Qutb-ud-din's subjects relied primarily on local architects and tra-ditions, which is why the Quwwat ul-Islam (Might of Islam) Mosque was built in the reddish-yellow sandstone typical of the area on the site of a col-umned hall characteristic of earlier Jain sanctuaries. Only the decoration and the bands of calligraphic script along the walls and façades are actu-ally traditional Islamic features. From the ruins of the large mosque rises the 72-m-high (236-ft) Qutb Minar, the tallest brick minaret in the world. Its base is around 15 m (49 ft) in diameter while the tip is just under 3 m (10 ft). Known for its red sandstone fluting, used here for the first time in India as a stylistic feature, the top two floors of Qutb Minar were destroyed by light-ning in the 14th century and rebuilt later in white marble.

THE RED FORT COMPLEX

Shah Jahan (Persian for "King of the World") was the fifth in a nota-ble series of Mughal rulers in India and was an energetic commissioner of buildings, including the Taj Mahal in Agra. Begun in 1639, it took just nine years to complete the Red Fort next to the Salimgarh Fort, which had been built by Islam Shah Suri back in 1546.

With magnificent portals (top: Lahore Gate), opulent watchtowers and defiant walls, the Red Fort was a clear symbol of Mughal power. The monumental complex comprises numerous palaces.

Together, these two grand edifices form the complex of the Red Fort in Old Delhi. This impressive struc-ture, which was plundered twice during its colored history – once in 1739 by Persian forces and then in 1857 by British troops –, owes its name to the imposing, 16-m-high (52-ft) sandstone walls that sur-round the complex. During sunset the red hues of the stone create a dazzling spectacle.

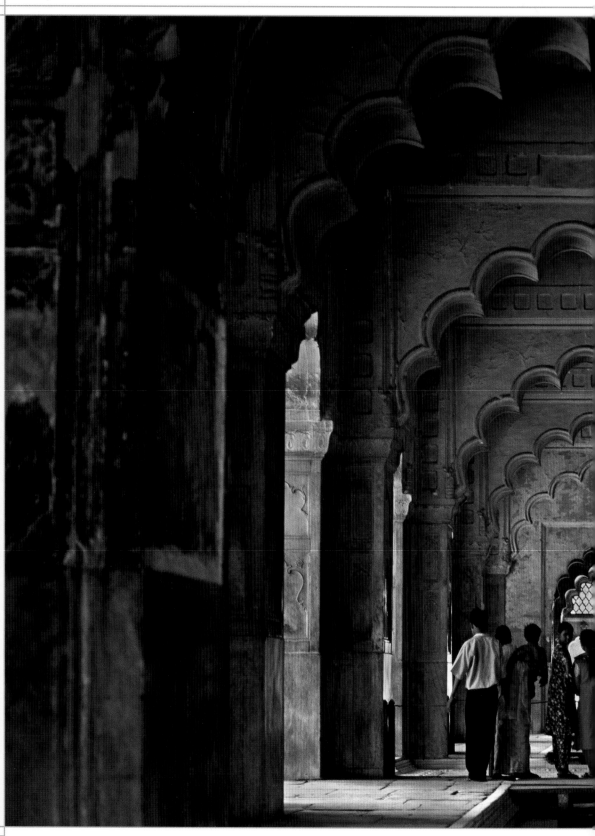

The famous Qutb Minar tower (left, in background) is the first Islamic building ever constructed on Indian soil. It is a stunning amalgamation of Indian-Hindu elements and Islamic architectural styles.

HUMAYUN'S TOMB

The works of Humayun, son of Babur, founder of the Mughal dynasty in India, were pivotal in the history of Mughal architecture. Although the security of his empire in India – he ruled between 1531 and 1556 – was initially less than ideal, the result was a boon. The young regent spent fifteen years in exile in Persia before returning, this time not just with a mighty army, but a host of master

Humayun's tomb was built on the initiative of his widow, Hamida Banu Begam, also known as Haji Begum. The Mughal ruler's final resting place (bottom) was not begun until 1570, some fourteen years after his death in 1556.

builders and artisans as well. His decision proved to be of great benefit to the architectural milieu on the Indian subcontinent, which flourished in the flood of new inspiration.

The Persian influence of his court is exemplified by the dome atop the high tambour, the gracefully arched alcoves and the spacious corridors of the tomb. The white marble and red sandstone façade also recalls Persian tradition.

AGRA

One of the most beautiful Islamic buildings in the world, the Taj Mahal (main picture) was constructed in Agra by the great Mughal emperor Shah Jahan as a tomb for his favorite wife, Mumtaz Mahal, who died in 1631. The complex is surrounded by an 18-hectare park.

THE RED FORT

Agra, situated on the west bank of the Yamuna River, owes its importance to the Mughal emperors, who built the Red Fort here (right, 2nd picture). The complex offers stunning views all the way to the Taj Mahal (right) and is named for the red sandstone from which it was constructed.

Begun in the year 1565 by Mughal Emperor Akbar, the Red Fort was later enlarged by Akbar's grandson, Shah Jahan. The buildings clearly demonstrate the different aesthetic preferences of the two rulers. Indicative of Akbar's imperial style are the Amar Singh Gate and the entire outer wall (below), while Shah Jahan preferred white marble.

TAJ MAHAL

The name of this famous white-marble architectural gem derives from Mumtaz Mahal, the endearing name of Shah Jahan's beloved wife, Arjumand Banu Begum, who lies buried there. The name means "Diadem Palace", or "Pearl of the Palace", and the edifice represents the zenith of a style that was initially developed in the architecture of the tomb of Humayun, one of Jahan's predecessors. At the end of long, terraced gardens and surrounded by grand water fountains, the perfectly symmetrical mausoleum

In the Taj Mahal's main chamber stand the two empty cenotaphs of Shah Jahan and his wife (top), adorned with passages from the Qur'an and decorative inlay work. Their actual tombs are found in the crypt below (bottom).

rises elegantly from a massive square plinth (right). The central domed tower sits on a high tambour in the Persian style and is surrounded by other domed pavilions. The wonderful façades, which are also designed in the Persian style, are oriented toward the four points of the compass while the four minarets accentuate the four corners of the plinth. The obvious Persian influence is thought to be the work of the lead archtiect, Isa Afandi, from Shiraz in the south-west of what is now Iran.

Agra is on the western bank of the Yamuna river and was the center of power for the Mughal emperors who build the Red Fort here. It is one of the largest in the world and provides fantastic views of the Taj Mahal (far left).

From the bay windows of the Hawa Mahal ("Palace of Winds") the ladies of the court were able to watch everyday life in the street through stone grillwork without being seen themselves (main picture).

TRIPOLIA AND JOHARI BAZAARS

It was the pink façades of the buildings that gave Jaipur its other name, the "Pink City". The capital of Rajasthan, Jaipur was founded in 1727 by Maharaja Sawai Jai Singh II, the 30th ruler of the Kachwaha dynasty and a man with a prominent place in his country's history books as a brilliant statesman, scholar and promoter of the arts. "Sawai" (meaning "One and a Quarter") is an honorary title for exceptional people that was bestowed on Jai Singh II early in his 43-year rule. In line with Hindu architectural tradition, Jaipur is laid out in a strict geometric plan. The residential blocks are aligned with the points of the compass while taking to consideration caste as well as astral constellations.

Aside from the tourist attractions you should also visit the bustling bazaars of the city, such as the Tripolia and the Johari bazaars, with everything from snake charmers, spices and vegetable merchants, and even precious stone traders in the jeweler's market at the end of Johari.

CITY PALACE

The complex of the town palace of Jaipur comprises several buildings and courtyards, all dominated by the multistory Chandra Mahal ("Moon Palace") from the 18th century. The former Mubarak Mahal ("Auspicious Palace") was built of sandstone in 1900 as a guesthouse and houses an exhibit of precious textiles including the finest silk and gold-embroidered brocade.

Large parts of the City Palace (top and center; bottom: the Hall of Private Audience, which the Maharaja still uses today) are open to the public, much like a museum.

Sileh Khana, a collection from the former arsenal, is one of the most valuable in India. In the Diwan-e-Khas ("Hall of Private Audience"), which the Maharaja still uses for receptions today, are two silver urns the Guinness Book of Records says are the largest silver vessels in the world. Also worth seeing is the royal collection of miniatures in the City Palace's Diwan-e-Aam (the former "Hall of Public Audience"). The Silver Throne is also here.

Jaipur is a feast for the senses, especially at the bazaars. Snake charmers invite spectators to an ancient dance while festively adorned elephants are proudly paraded through the lanes – in Jaipur tradition and modernity create a fascinating synthesis (left).

JANTAR MANTAR

Maharaja Sawai Jai Singh II built an observatory near the City Palace that was equipped with highly complicated astronomical instruments. The complex was constructed according to his own calculations. At first glance the huge sundials and measuring instruments seem futuristic even now, but Sawai Jai Singh II was a passionate mathematician, astronomer and astrologer. Having ascended to the throne

Jai Singh was of the opinion that the larger the instruments, the more accurate the results would be. Aside from the observatory in Jaipur (above) he had four more built in Delhi, Ujjain, Mathura and Varanasi.

at the tender age of eleven, he devoted himself to scholarship and knew all the current writings of his day. He read the works of Mirza Ulug Begh, for example, the famous astronomer and king of Samarkand. He studied Copernicus and Kepler and then wrote his own scientific compendium based on the measurements he made in his observatory. Astrologists even used some of his instruments when compiling horoscopes.

From left to right: Six Buddha figures, their right hands touching the earth, sitting at the entrance to the Temple of Swayambunath; the Golden Temple in Patan, founded in the 11th century; Durbar Square, bordered by the Archeological Museum and the Degutale Temple.

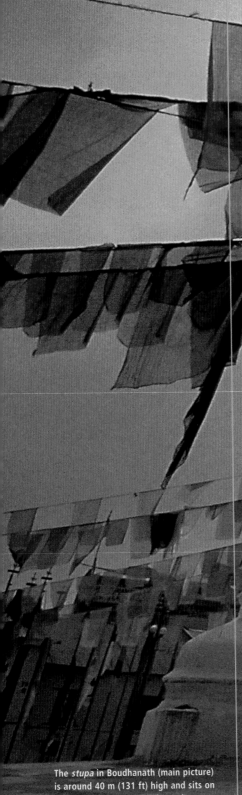

The *stupa* in Boudhanath (main picture) is around 40 m (131 ft) high and sits on a dome that in turn stands on three accessible plinths.

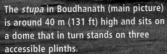

The fascinating ambience of the Kathmandu Valley is difficult to describe, but the pagoda-like roofs of the palaces, temples and houses, the wealth of exquisite carvings, and the opulence of the golden treasures in the temples all contribute greatly to the place. It is the whole package here that is so stunning, manifested in an atmosphere created by the inhabitants long before the first capital was founded in 723. Nepal's capital, the royal city of Kathmandu,

is at an elevation of 1,300 m (4,265 ft) and is the focal point of the valley. Situated at the confluence of the Bagmati and Vishnumati rivers, Kathmandu was an important trading center as early as the 10th century and one which, in competition with Patan and Bhaktapur, developed into one of Nepal's religious, cultural and political hubs before ultimately becoming the sole royal city.

The heart of the city is formed by Durbar Square, which the Nepalese

call "Hanuman Dhoka". It is the site of Buddhist and Hindu temples and shrines as well as the home of the former royal palace. The Malla kings and the kings of the Shah Dynasty resided here for centuries. The Boudhanath stupa, the largest sanctuary for Tibetan Nepalese people, is about 5 km (3 mi) outside of the heart of the city. The fascinating Swayambuna temple complex is situated in the north-west of the Old Town and is well worth a visit.

The highest mountain on earth is known to the Nepalese as Sagarmatha, or "Goddess of the Skies". The Tibetans call the mountain Chomolungma, "Mother Goddess of the Universe". Sagarmatha National Park, founded in 1976, not only contains three of the world's 8,000-m (26,000-ft) peaks (Mount Everest, Lhotse and Cho Oyu), but also has a number of 7,000-m (22,000-ft) and 6,000-m (19,0006-ft) summits.

The mountain's southern slopes are only snow-free for a short period in summer, a time when a variety of carnations, gentians and cruciferous plants blossom at elevations of up to 6,000 m (19,686 ft). Only very undemanding soil fungi are able to survive in the higher zones, while alpine plants such as edelweiss, irises and shrubs flourish in the lower regions. Deciduous and coniferous forests reach elevations of up to 4,000 m (13,124 ft). The national park is inhabited by some thirty mammal species and the skies are ruled by majestic raptors. The existence of the Yeti, however, still remains to be proven.

A breathtaking mountain landscape greets visitors in Sagarmatha National Park (main picture). In addition to the well-used southern route, a northern route from China takes mountaineers via the Rongbuk Valley to the top of Mount Everest (left) at 8,850 m (29,037 ft). Right: A view of Mount Everest and Lhotse from the Khumbu Valley.

Kamchatka lies in a subduction zone where the Pacific Plate pushes under the Eurasian Plate, a region that is part of the volcanic chain known as the Pacific Ring of Fire. It is home to a number of active stratovolcanoes such as Avachinsky (main picture).

KAMCHATKA

The Kamchatka Peninsula extends over a length of 1,200 km (746 mi) and is up to 480 km (298 mi) wide. It is situated between the Sea of Okhotsk in the west and the Pacific Ocean and the Bering Sea in the east, and is traversed by two parallel mountain ranges that are divided by the Kamchatka River Valley. The west or central range is dominated by extinct volcanoes, while the east range transforms into a plateau with a number of active volcanoes. Above: Karymsky volcano. Above right: Kronotsky volcano.

The west coast features expansive marshlands while the east is characterized by steep cliffs. The lower-lying zones are mostly covered with deciduous forest, the region providing a habitat for

many primeval indigenous plants. Its geographic location across the Pacific from the Americas meant that Kamchatka was a prohibited area until the end of the Cold War in 1990. This period provided ideal conditions for the local animal population to thrive relatively undisturbed. Its most spectacular representative is the Kamchatka brown bear (below, both photos), a subspecies of the brown bear that thoroughly enjoys the plentiful berries and fresh salmon on the peninsula.

WRANGEL ISLAND

them unique. Its mountainous terrain meant that it was never entirely covered in glaciers during the Ice Age, the result of which is that many plant and animal species exist here where elsewhere they have become extinct. Wrangel Island consequently has more than 400 species and sub-species of vascular plants alone, twice as many as in any other tundra region of comparable size. These also include twenty-three indigenous species that are the result of recent hybridization. The island is home to the world's largest population of Pacific walrus, numbering up to 100,000 specimens, and boasts the greatest density of polar bear caves in the world. Musk oxen also graze in the Arctic tundra landscape. Gray whales come here from Mexico to feed in these rich waters, and around 100 migrant bird species come here to breed. The large number of lemmings exhibit behavioral patterns that set them apart from other Arctic populations, while the reindeer have also adapted to the environmental conditions.

Wrangel Island – named after the Baltic German admiral and Siberian explorer Ferdinand von Wrangel – is situated well north of the Arctic Circle on the western edge of Chukchi Sea. It boasts a great diversity of geological formations and habitats, each with differing microclimates that make

The Chinese empire was ruled from Beijing's Forbidden City for nearly 400 years until 1911 when republican opposition movements triggered the demise of the monarchy. The emperor once occupied the Dragon Throne in the Hall of Supreme Harmony (main picture). The last emperor had to leave the palace in 1924, which now serves as a museum.

Beijing, which means "northern capital", was founded during the Jin Dynasty (1115–1234) before being laid to waste and rebuilt by the Mongols. The city was then once again built up by the Ming emperors between 1368 and 1420 based on plans from the original city. The town was to be a mirror image of the cosmos, whose laws were reflected in the city's layout. The old city center is formed by the Forbidden City, which straddles Beijing's main north-south axis. The modern center of Beijing is dominated by the vast Square of Heavenly Peace, named after the Gate of Heavenly Peace (Tiananmen), and is just to the south. It was here that Mao Zedong proclaimed the People's Republic of China in 1949.

On the square stand the Monument to the People's Heroes and the Mao Zedong Memorial Hall. On the western side it is bordered by the Great Hall of the People, and on the eastern side by the Museum of Chinese History and the Museum of the Chinese Revolution. When the square was built in 1958, it gave the capital city a socialist heart, a sort of "state cathedral".

Outside the Forbidden City is Chang'an Avenue, which runs from east to west across the city. The 40-km (25-mi) road is roughly 120 m (394 ft) wide at Tiananmen Square and was another of Mao Zedong's projects from the 1950s. Today, the glamorous boulevard is lined with government buildings, multinational company headquarters and modern hotels.

The inner-city districts essentially make up the historic center. So-called "hutong", houses built around courtyards and narrow alleyways, once characterized the older neighborhoods. Now only a few of them remain, for example around the Drum Tower, and these have been fully restored. Most

were demolished to make room for new roads and massive residential blocks. At the beginning of the socialist era, many inner-city districts were also peppered with iron and steel works, car and machine manufacturing facilities, locomotive and train car plants, and factories for the production of electronics and agricultural machines. These dramatic construction projects were meant to transform the bourgeois consumer town of the imperial age into a productive modern city. The result was that Beijing developed into the largest industrial center in China.

The historic ring of fortifications around the center was sacrificed for the enlargement of the city and construction of new roads, but the main axes of the road network follow the wall's former course, giving you an idea of the extent of the old imperial plan. Beijing also boasts a number of large parks. One of the best-known and largest – covering an area of 270 ha (667 acres) – is the park that houses the Temple of Heaven (Tian Tan), which contains the Hall of Prayer for Good Harvest and the Altar of Heaven. Both were built at the beginning of the 15th century.

For the Summer Olympic Games in 2008, the city's infrastructure was once again dramatically transformed, the most prominent new architectural feature being the national stadium. Designed by Swiss architects Herzog & de Meuron, it is 330 m (1,083 ft) long, 220 m (722 ft) wide, 69 m (227 ft) tall and has capacity for around 80,000 spectators. The stadium is north of the city about 9 km (6 mi) along the extension of the Forbidden City's northern axis in the Olympic Park, which was also newly constructed for the Games and covers an area of 800 ha (1,977 acres).

Insets, from left to right: The Imperial Palace, protected by a moat; the Gate of Heavenly Peace that led to the palace; the Hall of Prayer for Good Harvest, in the Temple of Heaven; the Zhichun Pavilion in Empress Cixi's Summer Palace, located on an island in Kunming Lake – a masterpiece of Chinese garden and landscape architecture near Beijing.

The original Great Wall – Wanli Chang Cheng – was built in the 5th century BC and largely made of clay. The brick reinforcement came later (main picture).

First mention of the building of a "long wall" on China's northern border was made in 214 BC. The territory had been united shortly before that by the Emperor Qin Shi Huang and the wall was intended to keep the nomadic people of the north at bay. Indeed, the problem of protecting Chinese interests became a recurring theme over the 1,900 years that followed.

The fortifications eventually fell into disrepair and were rebuilt on several occasions over the centuries. During the Ming Dynasty, in the 15th and 16th centuries, the wall was not only repaired but expanded to become a larger and more solid construction than ever before. The result is what we see today: a 6,000-km (3,728-mi) colossus, 2,000 km (1,243 mi) of

which are an average of 7-10 m (23-26 ft) high and 6 m (6.5 yds) wide between the Bohai Sea and the Yellow River. The watchtowers also served as soldiers' quarters and enabled the rapid communication of messages by means of beacons. The best-preserved and/or restored section of the wall is to be found near Badaling, north-west of Beijing.

With a length of more than 6,000 km (3,728 mi), the Great Wall (left near Jinshanling) is the largest structure on Earth. It was modified repeatedly for nearly 2,000 years. Ironically, the wall was never really able to protect the empire from attack.

The Bund, an embankment in the old
city center, offers a view of the Pudong
skyscrapers (main picture). Not only is
Shanghai growing horizontally, engulfing
the Yangtze Kiang Delta; it is also ex-
panding vertically, with the number of
high-rise buildings and skyscrapers
increasing on a daily basis.

the 16th century. Today a ring road still follows the oval outline of the wall. The Yu Garden in the northern part of the Old Town Nanshi is worth a visit. Modern Shanghai dates back to the Treaty of Nanjing (1842), which granted the right of domicile to Europeans. Below is one of the spectacular flyover constructions on the Huangpu River meant to cope

Shanghai roughly means "up or above the sea" due to its position at the confluence of two rivers at the coast. The Bund (above) is the embankment in the historical center of Shanghai. The city is home to China's most famous shopping mile, Nanjing Lu (left), and was once no more than a mooring place for junks that was then enclosed by a protective wall in

with ever increasing traffic from the Old Town to new Shanghai. Shanghai has become an important port town with multinational companies, banks, villas, factories and artisan quarters. The Huangpu District is on the north side of the Old Town and contains a number of interesting historical colonial buildings along the Bund. Above is the façade of the city museum.

HONG KONG

The name Hong Kong means "Fragrant Harbor". Right is the seat of the Legislative Council in front of the Bank of China tower. The rocky island at the mouth of the Pearl River was named as such on account of the incense sticks produced there. On the other side of the river is the Kowloon Peninsula which owes its name of "Nine Dragons" to the hilly landscape. Hong Kong became a British colony in 1842 and it was from here that the British ran their profit-

able opium trade, encroaching on Kowloon in 1860. The so-called Unequal Treaties of 1898 gave the British a 99-year lease on the New Territories along with 235 islands. The Crown Colony at the gateway to China eventually developed into one of the most densely populated and financially powerful trading hubs in the world. It has been a Special Administrative Region of China since July 1, 1997, a status that will last for 50 years, with its own currency, own economy and left-hand driving. "One nation – two systems" has since been the new order of things for Hong Kong.

Breathtaking: the view of Hong Kong's skyline in the nighttime sea of lights (main picture).

MACAU

Macau, situated in the Pearl River Delta, can be reached via speedboat from Hong Kong. After living under Portuguese rule for almost 500 years it was handed back to the People's Republic of China in December 1999.

The peninsula receives around six million visitors annually, mainly from Hong Kong, most of whom enjoy a stroll through the Old Town "where Portugal meets China". The central square Largo do Senado (above) with its wavy mosaic pavement is reminiscent of Portuguese towns.

Sightseeing attractions include Chinese temples juxtaposed with Christian churches and European-style palaces scattered among Chinese cemeteries. Some tourists come in search of rest and recuperation on the fine beaches of the islands of Taipe and Coloane, but the majority of visitors typically head straight for the multitude of floating casinos that constitute Macau's main source of income.

LHASA

Lhasa, meaning "place of the gods" and is capital of the Tibet Autonomous Region (TAR), lies on the Kyichu River at an altitude of almost 3,700 m (12,140 ft). Originally founded in the 7th century as the residential seat of the Tibetan kings (7th to 9th centuries), it later became the seat of government of the Lamaist theocracy in the

15th century, ruled by the Dalai Lamas. For hundreds of years, Lhasa was a "forbidden city" for foreigners.

The two-floor Jokhang Temple (above) dates from the 7th century and is situated in the heart of the Old Town. It is the oldest Buddhist

monastery in Tibet as well as a sort of Tibetan national sanctuary. All of the roads in Lhasa therefore lead to it. The temple is incidentally once again inhabited by practicing monks.

Almost as old as the Jokhang Temple is the Ramoche Temple (right) of the Chinese Princess Wencheng with its mighty outer walls. Unfortunately, the temple's many statues were either destroyed or confiscated by the Red Guards during the Cultural Revolution. With thirteen floors it rises 110 m (362 ft) above the city. Its façade alone is 360 m (1,000 ft) long, behind which are said to be 999 rooms

covering an area of 130,000 sq m (1,398,800 sq ft). Opposite is the grotto temple Drolha Lubuk with images of Buddhist deities alleged to have been created on their own. The Dalai Lama's summer palace, Norbulingka, in the west of Lhasa, is even larger.

KAILASH

"On seeing this snow-capped jewel our people leapt down from their saddles and bowed down on the ground," noted Sven Hedin after an excursion to Mount Kailash on Lake Manasarovar. The 6,714-m (22,029-ft) peak in Gangdisê Shan, the western section of the Tibetan Transhimalaya range, is believed to be the residence or throne of the gods – it is the holiest mountain in the world for Hindus, Buddhists, followers of the Ancient Tibetan Bön religion as well as those of the Ancient Indian Jain religion. Its summit may not be ascended and the 55-km (34-mi) circular route ("kora") is one of the most difficult pilgrimage paths in the world because of its altitude (around 5,000m/16,500 ft). It generally takes three to four days to complete. A kora corresponds to one revolution of the Wheel of Life and, according to the Tibetan faith, redeems all of the sins that the pilgrim has committed in his life to date. Especially pious Tibetans continually throw themselves onto the ground during the pilgrimage and measure the route with their own body length.

Main picture: The whitewashed section of the palace houses the administrative offices and storerooms, while the red section was the residence of the Dalai Lama until he fled in 1959. The entire complex has been a museum since then.

TOKYO

Roughly eight million people live in the Japanese capital and more than twelve million live in the greater prefecture. Tokyo is not only Japan's largest city, but also its most important economic and cultural center. This expansive metropolis is littered with skyscrapers that are visible from far and wide. Tokyo Tower, for example, (lit up in the main picture) is 333 m (1,093 ft) high, even taller than its role model, the Eiffel Tower in Paris.
Insets, left to right: the Shinjuku shopping district and the neon jungle of the main business and entertainment district, Ginza.

Main picture: The Rainbow Bridge spanning Tokyo Bay was completed in 1993 and measures 798 m (2,600 ft) in length – 570 m of which are between the two towers.

MOUNT FUJI

Japan's holy mountain (main picture) last erupted on December 16, 1707. The eruption lasted two weeks, forming an additional crater about halfway up as well as a second peak.

The islands of Japan form part of the so-called Ring of Fire, a string of seismically and volcanically active regions that encircles the Pacific Ocean. One of the many manifestations of this frequent activity is earthquakes, and Japan gets plenty of them. Although the Japanese use state-of-the-art technology in the construction of their buildings and transport network, even they are not able to combat the forces at work below the earth's surface.

Mount Fuji, a glorious result of the Ring of Fire's powers, rises up from the island in stoic silence. It is not only Japan's highest mountain, but also the country's undisputed icon – the pride of an entire nation. At a towering 3,776 m (12,38 ft), Fuji is crowned by a massive crater 600 m (1,900 ft) across and 150 m (492 ft) deep, with temples, cabins, a weather station and a radar station on its rim. Every year up to 400,000 people make the ascent in the summer season (July and August). There are five lakes – Motosu-ko, Shoji-ko, Sai-ko, Kawaguchi-ko and Ymanaka-ko – on the north side of the mountain.

HALONG

The marine landscape in Halong Bay – in the Gulf of Tonkin in northern Vietnam – comprises around 2,000 islands and features bizarre limestone cliffs. The wind, the weather and the tides have created an alluring natural work of art here (main picture).

The limestone cliffs in Halong can be up to 100 m (328 ft) high and most of them are covered with dense vegetation. Reminiscent of Chinese landscape paintings, these cliffs and mountains come in a wide variety of shapes ranging from broad-based pyramids and high, arched "elephant backs" to thin, towering needles of rock. The island landscape has often been perceived as more of a mythical spectacle than as a natural phenomenon: A dragon (Ha Long) descended from the mountains (or from heaven) is said to have created this natural wonder when it destroyed an army of enemy invaders with blows from its mighty tail – or was it that the dragon had been disturbed and therefore angered? The water displaced by the dragon as it dived under the sea then spilled into the resulting channels and canyons. The geological reality is somewhat more down-to-earth: Following the last Ice Age the coastal landscape forming part of the southwest Chinese limestone plateau sank and was flooded. It was erosion which ultimately formed the bizarre-shaped cones of rock.

Halong Bay is usually dominated by brisk shipping traffic (far left). Almost every one of the countless islands has its own name (left). Many of the grottoes and stalactite caves are only accessible at low tide (left).

HO CHI MINH CITY

While Hanoi is the country's political hub, Ho Chi Min City (in Vietnamese: Thanh Pho Ho Chi Minh, and formerly Saigon), is considered to be the industrial and economic heart of Vietnam. Modernization has indeed left its traces on the urban look and feel here, but the past still manages to shine through in some places. The colonial-style buildings, for example, and the roadside kiosks selling baguettes add a touch of the French colonial atmosphere to some of the city's neighborhoods. There are still oases of tradition in this vibrant metropolis, with monks praying in tranquil pagodas and puppeteers putting on shows in the parks. Like no other in Vietnam, Ho Chi Minh City embodies the dawning of a new era in the country. Above: City Hall, built in the French colonial style at the beginning of the 20th century.

One of the largest river deltas on earth is situated in southern Vietnam: the approximately 70,000-sq-km- (27,020-sq mile-) wide mouth of the Mekong River. The lotus flowers growing here (main picture) are seen as a symbol of purity because, although they flourish in muddy waters, their unique surface structure makes them appear completely clean. The pure blossoms growing out of the mud are the Buddhist symbol for the enlightened soul.

MEKONG DELTA

South of Ho Chi Minh City is a series of rolling hills that gives way to an almost perfectly flat expanse – the Mekong Delta. Rice paddy after rice paddy stretches between the countless channels where much of the daily activity takes place. Above: A farmer tends to his ducks. The delta is formed by the accumulated sedimentary deposits of the Mekong River, a process that is ongoing. The coastline along the river mouth extends further into the sea by around 80 m (262 ft) every year. This fertile land is used intensively for agriculture, making the region Vietnam's undisputed rice bowl (right).

This area is also one of the most densely populated in the country. The constant danger of flooding means that almost all of the houses here are built on stilts. Trading takes to the water during periods of flooding, when the river markets take place (left).

ANGKOR

Angkor Wat is the largest temple complex in Angkor, the former Khmer capital (main picture). The impressive ensemble with its distinctive prangs (temple towers) is approached from the main entrance along a stone embankment that is several hundred yards long.

The Khmer culture was strongly influenced by the Indian peoples that migrated to Southeast Asia in the first half of the first millennium. They prospered particularly after shaking off the domination of the Funan Empire (second to sixth centuries), which was also heavily influenced by Indian culture. The founder of the Khmer empire was Jayavarman II, who ascended the throne in 802. As the god king of Angkor with absolute religious and secular power, he acted as intermediary between heaven and earth. As a human being he lived in a palace and was venerated as a god in the temple. The Khmer rulers were Hindu-orientated until the beginning of the 13th century and were venerated in the form of Linga (the phallus of Shiva, creator and destroyer of the world), then later as an incarnation of Bodhisattva. Since the temple became the tomb of the god king after his death, every Khmer king built a sanctuary for himself. The most impressive complex is that of Angkor Wat, the temple of Suryavarman II (1113–50), under whom the Khmer culture reached its zenith.

Bangkok's Grand Palace (main picture) used to be a city in itself. The wealth of shades and shapes represented by the more than 100 buildings on the historical site continues to overwhelm visitors to this day.

CHINATOWN

Bangkok is vibrant, bustling, loud, chaotic and dazzling. More than ten million people live in the greater city and it is from here that the country is governed. The king lives here and all of the major companies are based here. It is also a city that never sleeps. Skyscrapers, luxury hotels and shop- ping malls make up modern Bangkok while the traditional monks, fortune- tellers and healers can be found in the temples along the river. The Chinese community in Bangkok has been here longer than Bangkok has been the Thai capital. The present-day Grand Palace grounds were home to a num- ber of Chinese traders even before King Rama I moved his capital from Thonburi to the opposite bank of the Chao Praya River in 1782. Forced to make way for the king's plans, the community withdrew to what is now Chinatown. A gate at Odeon Cir- cle marks the entrance to Yaowarat Road (with an express boat you can reach Chinatown from Ratchawong Pier) where it is best to continue on foot to explore the neighborhood.

GRAND PALACE UND WAT PHRA KAEO

The Siamese withdrew to Thonburi (now a district of Bangkok) after the destruction of their former capital Ayutthaya by the Burmese in 1767. It was here that Chao Phaya Chakri ascended to the throne in 1782 as King Rama I, thus founding the Chakri Dynasty, which is still the royal house of Thailand. It was in the first year of his regency that Rama I moved the seat of government to the opposite (east) bank of the river where the grounds of the Grand

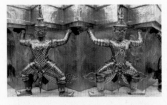

The Grand Palace grounds feature mythical creatures, demons and giants with "protective powers".

Palace now cover an area of 218,400 sq m (2,349,984 sq ft), enclosed on all four sides by a wall measuring 1,900 m (6,000 ft). Also on the east bank of the river was the village of Baan Makok, then largely inhabited by Chinese people, and from which the name conventionally used in the West, Bangkok, derives. The abbreviated form of the extended official name, Krung Thep, means "City of Angels". The most important sanc- tuary in the Grand Palace is the Wat Phra Kaeo Temple. Its architec- ture is based on the royal palace of Ayutthaya, a temple reserved solely for the king and his Buddhist ceremonies and which houses the most highly venerated Buddha statue in Thailand, the Emerald Buddha.

A kaleidoscope of Chinese culture in Bangkok (from far left): a calligrapher waits for customers; fresh piglet on a spit; shops sell their wares at street stalls.

WAT PHO

Not far from the Grand Palace is Wat Pho, the largest and oldest (16th century) temple complex in Bangkok with Thailand's largest statue of Buddha. The 45-m-long (150-ft) and 15-m-high (49-ft) statue (above) depicts Buddha shortly before his entry into Nirvana – a state of enlightenment (bodhi) in which the cycle of life (death, life and rebirth: samsara) is left behind. The historical Buddha achieved this state at the age of thirty-five and taught for another forty-five years thereafter.

WAT ARUN

The Temple of Wat Arun with its impressive tower and central sanctuary in which a seated Buddha invites the faithful to pray is one of the capital's most recognizable landmarks. The temple acquired its current name, the Temple of the Dawn, after King Taksin was rowed along the river one morning. It was Rama II, however, who then had an 86-m-high (282-ft) Khmer-style tower built over the original building. The main tower is flanked by four smaller towers. Thousands of Chinese pottery fragments were used to decorate the façade and while the result from up close tends to be somewhat dizzying, from a distance the details create a unique optical effect.

At 452 m (1,483 ft), the Petronas Towers (main picture and inset) are among the highest buildings in the world, not to mention Kuala Lumpur's most recognizable landmark. The 58-m (175-ft) Sky Bridge links the two towers at a height of 170 m (558 ft). The building was conceived by Cesar Pelli and officially opened in 1998.

KUALA LUMPUR

Malaysia's largest city is also the political and economic center of this Southeast Asian country. At this point, however, there is nothing about the capital today that is reminiscent of a "muddy estuary", which is what the name means. No other city in the country manifests so consistently the will of Malaysia to present itself internationally as an up-and-coming industrial nation, and it does so impressively with modern high-rise complexes such as the Petronas Towers (main picture and inset left), the administrative offices of multinational companies, banks and institutions as well as the numerous hotels.

Kuala Lumpur's appeal derives primarily from its vibrant ambience, the plentiful green spaces in the city center, the relaxing parks on the periphery, and particularly from the multicultural population mix – Chinese, Malay and Indian being the main ethnic groups – with their different cultures, traditions and ways of life.

The modern skyline is interspersed with the older parts of the city: the administrative buildings of the former British colonial powers and the villas of the tin barons as well as the traditional residential areas of the Indians and Chinese who live here.

BATU CAVES

The Batu Caves are around 15 km (9 mi) north of the capital on the road to Kuantan and are among the most frequently visited attractions in the Kuala Lumpur area. The enormous limestone caves form part of a labyrinth of rock openings and passageways that stretch over 1 km (0.6 mi).

The shrine (above) that was set up in the main cave back in 1892 has made this one of the most important pilgrimage destinations in the country for Malaysia's Hindu population.

Thousands of visitors travel to the Batu Caves in January and February every year when the two-day long Thaipusam Festival takes place. The highlight of the festivities is a procession of penitents who have metal hooks pushed into their backs and their chests (above).

Covering an area of 754,770 sq km (291,341 sq mi), the world's third-largest island – after Greenland and New Guinea – is one of the Greater Sunda Islands. Mount Kinabalu (main picture) is the highest peak in this very fragmented mountain region.

GUNUNG MULU

The largest cave complex on earth is tucked away in the spectacular mountain range of Gunung Mulu National Park, in the Malaysian province of Sarawak on Borneo. The formation of this craggy landscape began around thirty million years ago when pulverized volcanic rock formed the sand and sediment that made up what was then still a seabed. Coral and other marine fauna then formed the limestone over millions of years. Uplifting and a drop in sea levels about five million years ago then led to the creation of the mountain range that is today part of the protected national park territory and boasts stunning limestone formations like the 1,750-m-high (5,742-ft) Gunung Api. Directly adjacent to that limestone is a sandstone massif that makes up the highest peak, Gunung Mulu at 2,377 m (7,799 ft), after which the national park is named. The magnificent cave system, inhabited by a multitude of bats and insect species, was carved out by river erosion over the course of millions of years.

KINABALU

Kinabalu Park is situated in the Malaysian province of Sabah, at the northern end of the island of Borneo. It is known mainly for its primeval vegetation and for the highest mountain in Southeast Asia, Mount Kinabalu, which forms the impressive focal point of the park and – at 4,095 m (13,436 ft) – the highest mountain between the Himalayas and New Guinea. It is characterized by very diverse plant life that constantly changes between the different zones and

The rare flora and fauna on the island are protected by national parks. Top: Rainforest in Kinabalu Park. Middle and bottom: A ginger and a pitcher plant, respectively.

extends as far as the barren, rocky summit region. The tropical rainforest in the lowlands has more than 1,200 wild orchid species and many rhododendrons. The flowers range in hue from deep red to pale pink and white, followed at higher altitudes by montane forest with forty different types of oak overgrown with moss and ferns, coniferous forests and an alpine meadow and bush zone.

Gunung Mulu National Park, with its jagged limestone formations (left) and the gigantic cave complex (center: the Wind Cave) forms part of an impressive karst landscape. The Melinau River flows through the canyon of the same name (far left) in the park.

The Indonesian holiday paradise of Bali continues to fascinate visitors from all over the world. While the north and west are dominated by narrow, dark beaches, the south of the island boasts magnificent sandy beaches near Denpasar, picturesque bays and an overwhelmingly beautiful underwater world. The rice terraces in the center of the island are the work of generations of farmers who made the steep slopes arable. Tanah Lot, one of the island's most scenic temples, is located on an offshore rocky outcrop. The romantic Pura Ulun Danu Bratan temple complex (above right with traditional carved deity masks), is situated on the southwestern shores of Bali's Lake

Bratan and, founded in the 17th century, is dedicated to the water goddess Dewi Danu. The "Mother of all Balinese temples", Pura Besakih, is situated atop the 3,142-m (10,309-ft) active volcano, Gunung Agung. Every clan and every professional category is represented by its own temple here. The holiest of complexes, it is accessible only to Hindus. The

summit of Gunung Agung offers a magnificent view of the adjacent island of Lombok. Visitors will find temples and palaces on the west coast of Lombok that are similar to Bali as well as picture-postcard sandy palm beaches. There are impressive coral reefs around the island as well, making snorkelling or diving trips here a unique experience.

Main picture: Balinese dancers wear
elaborate makeup for their "Homage
to the gods" dance.

The land of "Dreamtime"… and dreamy landscapes. From the azure blue Barrier Reef to the dark green rainforests of the Wet Tropics, from the glowing red rock monoliths of Uluru National Park to the yellow-gold sand dunes of Nambung National Park, the fifth continent mirrors the earth's fascinating variety. The view of the Caroline Oslands (main picture), the largest group of islands in Micronesia, is also unforgettable. They comprise 963 islands and atolls, most of which are volcanic in origin. There is archeological evidence of early settlement here.

SIMPSON DESERT, ULURU AND KATA TJUTA, NITMILUK

While Uluru (aka Ayer's Rock, main picture, top) is a single formation with a circumference of about 10 km (6 mi), Kata Tjuta comprises thirty-six smaller, rounded domes (main picture, bottom).

SIMPSON DESERT

Large, rusty-red sand dunes extend up to 300 km (186 mi) to the north-west and seem to glow in the evening light. They are the main feature of Simpson Desert National Park, which contains the longest parallel dunes in the world. It was only mapped from the air in 1929. The first non-vehicular crossing was undertaken forty-four years later, in 1973, and another four years later by writer Robin Davidson, who started in South Australia on camelback. He managed to find the Oodnadatta Track, a stretch of outback covering more than 615 km (382 mi) that was named after the tiny outpost of Oodnadatta on the south-western edge of the Simpson Desert.

ULURU AND KATA TJUTA

The Uluru and Kata Tjuta National Park is situated in a vast area of sparse, dry savannah. The iconic red rocks were discovered almost simultaneously in October 1873 by the two explorers William Gosse and Ernest Giles. They named Ayers Rock after Henry Ayers, the prime minister of South Australia at the time – to which the Northern Territory then belonged.

The formation of Uluru (the Aboriginal name for Ayers Rock) began around 570 million years ago and is related to the geological crea-

Uluru – "shady place" – is what the Aborigines call their sacred mountain (top and bottom). The monument was returned to them in 1985 and forms the heart of a national park that also encompasses the rock formations of Kata Tjuta, meaning "many heads".

tion of the entire Australian continent. Unlike the surrounding rock, the cliffs are very resistant and weathered very slowly, today towering above the plain as magnificent petrified witnesses of the Paleozoic. Despite the inhospitable surroundings, the Anangu have been living in this area for thousands of years; for the Aborigines this is the meeting place of their mythical ancestors in Dreamtime.

Even a desert as seemingly inhospitable as the Simpson Desert (far left: a satellite image) is not lifeless. Pictures, from right to left: A python; a thorny devil, which eats mainly ants but can let the morning dew run into their mouths via grooves in their skin; and a collared lizard.

NITMILUK

The main attraction in this national park roughly 30 km (19 mi) north-east of the town of Katherine is the stunning system of canyons, commonly known as Katherine Gorge, formed by the river of the same name. Over millions of years the Katherine River has worked itself deep into the Arnhem Plateau over a stretch of 12 km (7 mi), creating canyons as deep as 13 to 100 m (43 to 328 ft). Some of the more spectactular spots can be viewed by boat or canoe but during the rainy season the Katherine River becomes a raging torrent and can therefore only really be negotiated

A canoe trip through Katherine Gorge (top) in Nitmiluk National Park is a unique experience. Inhabitants of the area include the Argus monitor (bottom). From the water you can get amazing views of the up to 100-m-high (328-ft) rock faces.

safely during the dry season (April to October). During this time, however, it is more a series of separate pools between which you will have to carry your canoes over the dried-out rapids. Anyone who goes to this trouble will be able to access a total of nine gorges and enjoy the wild beauty of the glorious red-rock walls. Tourist boats are limited to the first four gorges.

The structure of the Great Barrier Reef appears clearly in the satellite images of Princess Charlotte Bay and Cape Melville (right). The longest living coral reef on earth extends from the Tropic of Capricorn to the mouth of the Fly River (New Guinea). The reef, comprised of around 2,500 individual reefs and 500 coral islands, follows more than 2,000 km (1,243 mi) of the north-eastern coast of Australia at a distance from the mainland of 15 to 200 km (9 to 124 mi).

The masterbuilders of this natural wonder are coral polyps (below, middle) who live together with blue-green algae. The polyp larvae hatch in the spring and are already able to swim at birth. They then attach themselves to the reef close to the surface of the water, slowly developing their skeletons and forming colonies with other members of their species. After a short while they die off and their calcium carbonate tubes are

ground into fine sand. The algae then "cake" the sand into a new reef layer on which new young polyps are able to settle the following year. This is how the reefs and islands have developed over thousands of years. Around 1,500 species of fish live in the waters around the reef, including the bright clownfish (below, left), made famous in the film *Finding Nemo*, the gray reef shark (below, right), pomacentrids, manta rays and stingrays. The reef is also home to thousands of bird, coral and invertebrate species.

One of the loveliest sections of the Great Barrier Reef is off the Whitsunday Islands (main picture). Coral polyps have been working on the earth's largest natural "construction" for around 8,000 years.

SYDNEY

The view of Sydney with the bridge and the opera house is famous throughout the world. In 1955, a largely unknown Danish architect named Jörn Utzon won the contest for the opera house design. He submitted no more than sketches as plans and it was only much later, in 1959, once the foundations had been built, that any thought was given to how the roof was actually to be structured. In the end it cost a total of 102 million Australian dollars instead of the intended seven million.

BLUE MOUNTAINS

In 1836, a prominent witness to the beauty of the Blue Mountains, Charles Darwin, described the view from the rocky ledges as "fantastic". His opinion is likely to be confirmed by anyone venturing into Sydney's hinterland. Despite their low altitude of between 600 and 1,000 m (1,969 and 3,2181 ft), the mountains are very rugged, with much of the area still more or less untouched by humans. Above: A waterfall in the Valley of the Waters.

MUNGO

The landscape of Mungo National Park (above) was overgrazed by sheep in the 19th century, lumber was taken for houses and barns, and the loose soil was then carried away by the wind. But 15,000 years ago the entire area was under water and traces of settlements around 40,000 years old have now been found along the shores of the former lake – including petrified human remains. DNA analysis indicated they are the oldest traces of Homo sapiens in Australia.

Sydney Harbour Bridge (main picture) was built by around 1,400 laborers. Paul Hogan, alias Crocodile Dundee, was one of them. The view of the city from the bridge is well worth seeing.

TASMANIA

Australia's largest island is also its smallest state. Typical for Tasmania are the steep steps, the so-called "tiers", tablelands which drop down to the coast (main picture: at South Cape). Large areas of the island remain largely untouched even today.

FLINDERS ISLAND

Flinders Island lies to the north-east of Tasmania in the Bass Strait and was named after surveyor Matthew Flinders who was here as a cartographer in 1797. It forms part of the Furneaux Group – thought to be the remains of a former land bridge between Tasmania and the Australian continent – and has something of a dark past. The indigenous inhabitants of Tasmania were exterminated within just a few decades of British colonial rule. Strzelecki National Park, which affords a view of Cape Barren Island, is situated in the south.

EAST COAST

In contrast to the largely uninhabited west coast, Tasmania's east coast is more easily accessible and can be reached on the Tasman Highway. Part of the east coast is formed by the Tasman Peninsula, where the former Port Arthur prison camp is situated. There are five important protected areas along the east coast: Tasman National Park (above the dolerite cliffs off the coast), Maria Island National Park, Freycinet National Park with Wineglass Bay, Douglas Apsley National Park, and Mount William National Park, virtually on the northern tip of the island.

TASMANIAN WILDERNESS

This protected area essentially includes the national parks of Cradle Mountain–Lake St Clair, Southwest, Franklin Lower Gordon Wild Rivers as well as three smaller areas. The wild, romantic landscape was formed by glaciers during the last ice age and is characterized by a great many lakes and waterfalls. Abel Tasman, the first white man to set foot on the island on December 2, 1642, thought it too bleak for settlement. The island receives up to 2,500 mm (98 in) of annual rain, however, facilitating the growth of temperate rainforests (left). They look familiar from a distance and close up we recognize them: a place of sub-Antarctic and Australian shapes. Tasmania's most famous animals are the unique duck-billed platypus and the Tasmanian devil (above).

"Middle Earth" in New Zealand: Mount Ngauruhoe's mighty, flat volcanic cone (main picture) was the model for "Mount Doom" in Peter Jackson's internationally successful film adaptation of J.R.R Tolkien's "Lord of the Rings".

TONGARIRO

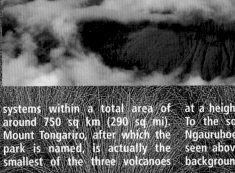

Tongariro, the oldest national park in New Zealand, was donated by New Zealand's original Polynesian population, the Maori. In 1887, Chief Te Heuheu Tukino gave the Maori's sacred land around the Tongariro volcano to the New Zealand government with the specific condition that it be protected for all humankind. Situated in the heart of New Zealand's North Island, the national park encompasses three active volcano systems within a total area of around 750 sq km (290 sq mi). Mount Tongariro, after which the park is named, is actually the smallest of the three volcanoes at a height of 1,968 m (6,457 ft). To the south of that is Mount Ngauruhoe at 2,290 m (7,513 ft), seen above with Tongariro in the background. It is the most active of the three volcanoes in this national park. The third, Ruapehu (left), comprises several cones and is the highest mountain on the North Island at 2,797 m (9,177 ft).

EGMONT

Egmont National Park encompasses the last primeval forest areas around the volcanic mountain Taranaki, which has been dormant for the last 300 years.

Asphalt roads bring visitors to rest points at an altitude of roughly 1,100 m (3,609 ft) above sea level, while short hiking trails provide access to fabulous, fairy-

tale-like forests. For the Maori, the snow-covered peak of New Zealand's most famous mountain symbolizes the sacred heads of their ancestors. It was here that

the bones of leaders who had fallen in battle were laid to rest while legends about murderous giants and wicked elves kept intruders out. Every Maori tribe had its "own" mountain and a volcanic eruption was seen as a sign of wrath or as a signal to take up arms. A victory could also cause the mountain to swell with pride. When two tribes made peace after battle their mountains were also symbolically wed.

AORAKI/MOUNT COOK

Aoraki/Mount Cook National Park, which covers a vast area of about 700 sq km (270 sq m), is home to all of New Zealand's 3,000-m (9,843-ft) peaks, with the exception of Mount Aspiring. The highest of the peaks is Mount Cook at 3,754 m (12,317 ft), known to the Maori as "Aoraki", which can be roughly translated as "cloud piercer". A rock slide in 1991 reduced the height of Aoraki to 3,754 m (12,317 ft), but it still towers a few hundred meters over its number two, Mount Tasman, at 3,498 m (11,477 ft).

Once the training ground for Sir Edmund Hillary, the Auckland-born mountaineer who managed the first ascent of Mount Everest,

Mount Tasman is accessible from the east via a 60-km (37-mi) access road that takes you along the shores of Lake Pukaki. New Zealand's most formidable ice field, the Tasman Glacier, is 29 km (18 mi) long, up to 3 km (1.8 mi) wide and nearly 600 m (1,969 ft) thick in places.

In addition to the Kea mountain parrot, the flora and fauna in this national park include rare falcon and owl species, while the star amongst the plants is the Mount Cook Lily. The hiking trail through Hooker Valley takes you across the valley floor (below) and crosses the Hooker River glacier by means of two rope bridges. The routes over ice and snow are naturally more strenuous.

WESTLAND

Because the Fox and Franz Josef glaciers are easily accessible and draw around 350,000 visitors annually, most of the other routes in the Westland National Park (main picture: Lake Matheson) are usually deserted.

It is out on the bright sheets of ice that the mountain world of the Westland National Park reveals its full allure. Its magnificent main glaciers, Franz Josef in the north and Fox (above) in the south, flow down the steep valleys from the main alpine ridge around Mount Cook and end in the rainforests around 13 km (8 mi) from the coast. Both glaciers had been receding consistently for four decades before advancing once again in the 1980s when the weight of heavy snowfalls on the main plateau pushed the Franz Josef Glacier edge down the valley at an average of 6 m (20 ft) a week. The Fox Glacier only managed 1 m (3 ft) in the same period. Although both glaciers are again receding at present and are far removed from their historical peaks (indicated along the route with the dates), the Franz Josef Glacier today extends 600 m (1,969 ft) further into the valley than it did in 1982.

Papua New Guinea (above: stilt villages on the Sepik River) is only about 150 km (93 mi) off the Cape York Peninsula of northern Australia. The country comprises roughly 85 percent of the eastern part of the island of New Guinea while the rest is spread over a further 600 islands, the largest of which are New England and New Ireland.

The substantial differences in elevation – one quarter of the country lies above 1,000 m (3,281 ft) – account for the vast range of vegetation that exists here. Oak trees, bay trees and conifers dominate the mountains, while the low-lying areas boast palms, climbing plants, ferns and orchids.

Papua New Guinea's cultural diversity is also unique on the planet: Around 95 percent of the population is made up of Melanesians, who are divided into ever smaller clans that speak several hundred, mutually unintelligible languages. There are also small groups of Papuans (the island's indigenous inhabitants), splinter groups from Micronesia and Polynesia, and about 20,000 foreigners.

The Western Highland Province is inhabited by hundreds of traditional clans who gather in the provincial capital Mount Hagen every August for a festival of song and dance (below: festival participants sporting their white and orange stripes).

Main picture: Papua New Guinea's largest ethnic population is the Huli, who are often referred to as "wig men" on account of their elaborate headdress. Their abundance of adornments and vibrant body painting are an expression of their consummate creative skills, which have always impressed explorers and visitors.

Bora Bora Lagoon (main picture) is the stuff that South Sea dreams are made of. The "Pearl of the Pacific" is famous for its mighty volcanic stacks that jut out of the blue and turquoise sea.

FIJI ISLANDS

The majority of Fiji's islands are relatively close to each other compared to other similiar groups in the South Pacific: within a radius of only 250 km (155 mi). The two main islands, Viti Levu and Vanua Levu, are volcanic and feature high, jagged ranges that dot the interior. The climate is predominantly tropical, with the windward side on the south-east recording a hefty 3,000 to 5,000 mm (118 to 197 in) of annual rainfall. This feeds the dense mountain forests as well as the coastal mangroves and coconut palms. Meanwhile, less than half as much rain falls in areas protected from the wind. There, grasses dominate the landscape and cane sugar is a major crop. The largest island, Viti Levu, boasts bubbling hot springs and a number of rivers. Fiji is also famous for its coral reefs, which lie at a great range of depths. The islands are a mecca for soft coral diving.

The first humans are said to have settled on Fiji at least 3,500 years ago. What is unclear, however, is where these people came from.

FRENCH POLYNESIA

The six archipelagoes of French Polynesia (Society, Tuamotu, Marquesas, Austral, Gambier and Bass) are located in eastern Polynesia and their 118 islands cover a total area of about 4.5 million sq km (1,737,000 sq mi). One of the largest of the thirteen Marquesa islands is Nuku Hiva, which has dramatic coastal formations that drop nearly vertically into the sea. Its highest volcano is Poitanui on Uapu (1,232 m/4,042 ft). The Tuamotu archipelago, which consists exclusively of atoll reefs, is more than 1,000 km (621 mi) to the south-west.

A dance performance in Papeete, French Polynesia. Open your eyes and your heart, and you will soon understand why Polynesian culture reached its zenith on these islands.

The best-known island group is the Society Islands, some 1,500 km (932 mi) west of Tuamotu. It comprises by far the largest island, Tahiti, as well as Raiatea, Bora Bora and Moorea.

Tahiti, in the geographic heart of Polynesia, is also the economic and cultural center of the French overseas territory. Tahiti was made a French protectorate in 1842, and in 1880 a French colony. The other islands were taken into French possession by 1881. The islands are divided into the "Windward Islands" and "Leeward Islands", depending on their exposure to the south-east trade winds. Volcanic in origin, they boast lush tropical vegetation surrounded by rich coral reefs.

In 1643, Abel Tasman was the first European to discover the Fiji Islands. Their bright white beaches and turquoise-colored sea attract not only beach bums and divers, but favorable swells also offer excellent conditions for surfing (left).

The solitude of the sand desert, the fires of the Virunga volcanoes, the raging waters of Victoria Falls, the majesty of Mount Kilimanjaro, the pyramids of Egypt, the palaces of Morocco, and the monasteries of Ethiopia. The Serengeti, Masai Mara, Okavango Delta, Chobe. Tuareg, Nuba, Samburu, Zulus. The diversity in Africa is hard to beat. Main picture: Quiver trees, endemic aloe plants in the southern Namibian desert.

FEZ

In 809, Idris II made Fez an imperial town. The city has since grown into a modern metropolis, but in the Old Town (main picture: Bab Bou Jeloud Gate), time seems to have stood still.

KAIRAOUINE MOSQUE

The green-tiled roofs of Kairaouine Mosque (above) can clearly be made out in the sea of houses in Fez el-Bali's medina. Morocco's second-largest sacred building, it was constructed in Moorish style, with 270 supporting columns.

TANNERY QUARTER

Visitors here can get a glimpse of the densely packed vats filled with natural tannins and dyes (above) as well as of the hard physical labor of the tanners. The animal hides are cleaned, soaked, hung up to dry and then dyed.

ROYAL PALACE

The gate to the Royal Palace in "New Fez", founded by the Marinid sultans to the south-east of Fez el-Bali, features seven beautifully gilded brass doors that are framed by zellij polychrome tiles and stucco (above).

THE OLD TOWN

Fez was founded by the Idrisid rulers as a twin city on an important trading route from the Sahara Desert to the Mediterranean Sea. The oldest part of the town, Fes el-Bali, was settled by Andalusian refugees from the Moorish region of Spain as well as by families from present-day Kairouan in Tunisia. The Kairaouine Mosque, which goes back to these settlers, provides room for more than 20,000 worshippers. It is also the center of the highly regarded university that was founded in the year 959. Andalusia Mosque also dates back to the early days of the town. Fes el-Bali is surrounded by impressive city walls featuring twelve unique gates.

Fez experienced a time of great prosperity in the 14th century under the Marinid rulers. The Royal Palace, the Bou Inania Medersa and the Mellah (the Jewish Quarter) all date from that time. Qur'anic schools, mosques and the tombs of the Marinids testify to the importance of this part of town, Fès el-Djedid. The French conquered the city in 1911.

Although it is not the capital city, Fez is still considered the spiritual and cultural center of Morocco. The Old Town features partly covered alleyways and a number of stylish minarets (left).

NEJJARINE SQUARE

Nejjarine Square, near the carpenters' souk, has one of the most beautiful fountains in the city (above). To the left you enter the Nejjarine Foundouk, the former Inn of the Carpenters and today the Nejjarine Museum of Wood Arts & Crafts.

TOMB OF MOULAY IDRISS II

The Zaouia (shrine) of Moulay Idriss II in Fez is still one of the most important pilgrimage sites in Morocco. The complex of buildings includes a delightful mosque and a courtyard. Precious materials were used in the ornamentation (above).

MADRASSA ES-SHARIJ

The Marinids are responsible for some of Morocco's most famous madrassas – religious schools. One, the Madrassa es-Sharij, was named after the large fountain shaped like a water basin in the middle of its magnificent inner courtyard (above).

MARRAKESH

The minaret of the Koutoubia Mosque is the best-known landmark in Marrakesh, the southernmost of Morocco's four former imperial cities. The oasis city was once an important center for trans-Saharan trade and served as a capital for the rulers of several dynasties.

Among the structures dating from the early period of the medina, the town walls have been very well preserved. Overall, they cover roughly 10 km (6 mi) and contain ten gates and more than 200 towers, some of which were added later. The mosque and its minaret, built in the year 1153 by the Almohad sultans, is one of the most attractive buildings in the city. Together with the Giralda of Seville and the Hassan Tower of Rabat, the nearly 80-m (262-ft) masterpiece is a mixture of Spanish and Moorish architecture that quickly became a model for min-

arets all around the country. Just behind the beautiful mosque is the tomb of the city's founder, Yusuf ibn Tashfin.

Visitors enter the ancient fortified town of the Almohads, referred to as a casbah, via the 12th-century Bab Agnaou, Marrakesh's most beautiful city gate. Another architectural gem is the Ben Youssef Madrassa, built in the 14th century under the "Black Sultan" – a Marinid ruler. The 16th century was another period of great building activity. Dating back to this period are the elaborate Saad tombs (above). The inner rooms of the necropolis are splendidly decorated with cedar, stuccowork and mosaics. In addition to several palaces – the Royal Palace, Bahia Palace (top left), the ruins of El Badi – the souks (insets, opposite page) and the main market square, Djemaa el Fna (main picture), with its traveling entertainers are among the top attractions in Marrakesh. The Agdal and Menara Gardens outside the city (above) are also worth seeing.

Located in the heart of Marrakesh is Djemaa el Fna, the "Square of the Beheaded". After sunset, hundreds of people crowd around the food stalls, snake charmers, storytellers and acrobats (main picture).

THE HIGH ATLAS, CASBAH TRAIL

Main picture: A panoramic view of the Todra River Valley, which rises in the High Atlas. In the language of the Berbers, "ouzuoud" means "olives", after which the 110-m (361-ft) Ouzoud Waterfalls were named (opposite page).

THE HIGH ATLAS

Rising up between Middle Atlas and Anti-Atlas, the High Atlas range forms the border between fertile Morocco and the desert. Its highest mountain is Jbel Toubkal (4,167 m/13,672ft). The Cascades d'Ouzoud are a spectacle of incomparable beauty and Morocco's most impressive waterfalls.

In the deep, narrow Todra and Dades Gorges of the High Atlas, farmers make use of every tiny scrap of fertile land. The Todra River cuts its course through steep rock faces and extends from the High Atlas down to the Dades Valley, where its banks are lined by thousands of palm trees. The cool canyon is popular among rock climbers and hikers.

THE CASBAH TRAIL

Thanks to its many clay fortresses, the Dades Valley is also known as the "Route of 1,000 Casbahs". At the turn of the 20th century, it was El Glaoui in particular, the infamous pasha of Marrakesh, who secured his sphere of influence by commissioning such casbahs to billet his troops.

The summits of the High Atlas are covered with snow until well into the spring (far left). In the deep ravines (left, a meandering river) near the "Route of 1,000 Casbahs", farmers make use of every available scrap of fertile land to grow tomatoes, alfalfa and millet in their tiny fields.

KAIROUAN

The town of Kairouan, around 150 km (230 mi) south of Tunis, was founded in about 670 by the Uqba ibn Nafi of the Omayyad Dynasty as an outpost for the conquering Arab army. The mosque named after him is the oldest in North Africa and one of the most attractive religious structures in Tunisia (above). The town experienced its heyday in the ninth century during the rule of the Aghlabids Dynasty of emirs.

TUNIS

Around two million people live in greater Tunis where the suburbs spread like the tentacles of an octopus along the Bay of Tunis, from Bou Kornine Mountain to the saline lakes of the lagoon. The history of the city goes back to the ninth century BC. When the Phoenicians founded Carthage, a settlement established by the indigenous Numidians and originally known as Tunes already existed there. It wasn't until 894, however, that Tunis finally became an important capital during Aghlabid rule. A walk through the medina – the largest preserved

Old Town in North Africa – takes visitors past whitewashed houses with splendidly mosaic and tiled façades (below), past mosques and minarets and through the expansive colonnaded *souks*, or bazaars. The Zitouna Mosque (left) in the heart of the city is surpassed in size and importance only by the Great Mosque in Kairouan. It owes its name to an olive tree that once stood there and is supposed to have had miraculous healing powers.

Kairouan is still one of the most important Islamic centers in North Africa. Especially worth seeing is the Great Mosque in the Old Town whose prayer hall is structured by Roman columns (main picture).

EL DJEM

The Roman amphitheater of El Djem in Central Tunisia was built in about AD 230 and remodeled as a fortress after the withdrawal of the Romans. During the seventh century it served as a sanctuary for the female Berber leader Dahia al-Kahina in her futile battle against the Arab conquerors. Measuring 148 by 122 m (450 by 375 ft) and a good 40 m (131 ft) high, the massive oval building can accommodate 30,000 spectators and is still one of the largest and best-preserved amphitheaters in the entire former Roman Empire.

CAIRO

"He who has not seen Cairo has not seen the world," it says in the tales of One Thousand and One Nights. Today, nearly one in four of the just under 70 million Egyptians live Africa's largest city. The glitter of the metropolis on the Nile may have faded a little since the days of Scheherazade, but Cairo is much more than just the undisputed political, spiritual and economic heart of the country. It is also the epitome of an Oriental fairytale city and as such it continues to fascinate visitors.

Al Qahira – the "Triumphant One", a name that was later corrupted to Cairo by Italian merchants, was founded in the year 969 by Shiite rulers, the Fatimids, near the ancient Arabic settlement of Fustat. Initially it served as a palace city, but it was Saladin, founder of the Ayyubid dynasty, who finally opened the royal enclave to the public.

OLD CAIRO

The district of Old Cairo is primarily inhabited by Copts, the Christian descendants of the ancient Egyptians and boasts more than 2,000 years of history. During the reign of the emperors

Hadrian and Trajan, a Roman fortress named Babylon already controlled transport on the Nile. In 642, the Muslim conqueror Amr Ibn el-As erected the encampment which eventually developed into the first Arabic capital. One slightly peculiar sight is the Al-Moallaqa Church, which is dedicated to the Madonna (left and right) and boasts more than 100

icons, some dating back more than a thousand years. It owes its epithet, "the Hanging One", to the fact that – at least visually – it appears "suspended" above the entrance to the historic Babylon.

AL-AZHAR

The Al-Azhar Mosque and University rise gloriously out of the heart of the Old Town. It was named after Fatima, the Prophet's daughter, who is said to have been so beautiful that she was known as al-Zahra, "the Most Flourishing and Shining". The intricate complex of buildings comprises a place of worship, a madrassa, or Qur'anic school, and students' hostels as well as five

minarets. For more than 1,000 years it has been the intellectual and power center for the entire Arab and Muslim world; somewhat similar to the relationship Oxford and the Sorbonne have with the Vatican. A subdued bustle usually prevails in the interior courtyard here, which is encircled by alabaster columns. The adjoining prayer hall was once used for lectures.

KHAN EL-KHALILI

Khan el-Khalili, Cairo's vast *souk*, or market, is situated between Muski Street and the Hussein Mosque and attracts visitors like a giant magnet. It was named after a Mamluk stable master who some 600 years ago had a large trading estate built here. Nearby was the spice market where merchants from Arabia,

Persia and India traded exotically scented goods. Today, the range of wares consists largely of trinkets for credit card-wielding tourists. As far as the overall atmosphere is concerned, however, the maze of narrow and mostly covered alleyways still conjures up the authentic atmosphere of a large bazaar.

MOHAMMED-ALI

The Mosque of Mohammed Ali (1824–57), with its slender minarets and mighty vaulted dome, stands out in all senses of the term. As the defining silhouette of the Old Town, it is perched high atop Citadel Hill. Its walls are covered in alabaster, a mar-

ble-like plaster that gave the mosque its other name – the Alabaster Mosque. Mohammed Ali (1769–1849), born in what is now Macedonia, is buried in the western corner of the domed Byzantine edifice. He is revered as the founder of modern Egypt.

Three thousand years and thirty-one dynasties are on display in the fifty rooms of the Egyptian Museum. Thousands of steles,

EGYPTIAN MUSEUM

reliefs and sarcophagi, jewelry, small houses, models of ships and other sacrificial offerings command respect and admiration from every visitor. The featured attractions are the death masks of the ancient Egyptian pharaohs (left: the mask of Tutankhamun).

Main picture: Cairo is also known as the "City of 1,000 Minarets": Here the towers of the 14th-century Sultan Hassan Mosque mingle with the adjacent Er Rifai Mosque dating back to 1912.

LUXOR

The temple city of Karnak, a necropolis on the west bank of the Nile, combines with the town of Luxor on the east bank to form a focal point of ancient Egyptian culture. They are the main attractions of any visit to Upper Egypt. The foundation stone for the central temple complex, which stands in the heart of the urban area right on the promenade, was laid as early as 1380 BC by Amenophis III (or Amenhotep III).

A symbol of power in the New Kingdom, the temple was dedicated to the trinity of gods in Thebes: Amun, Mut and Chons. Today it still presents an amazing wealth of giant statues, obelisks, pylons and papyrus columns all lined up over a length of 260 m (853 ft). The smaller artifacts from there and other excavation sites have all been taken to the local museum where they are expertly displayed.

KARNAK

For many centuries, the temple complex of Karnak (above), north of Luxor's city center, was Egypt's main spiritual sanctuary. It is dedicated to Amun, the "Hidden One", an ancient divinity mentioned as far back as the pyramid texts of the Old Kingdom but who did not become the imperial god Amun-Ra of Thebes until 2000 BC. The complex originally boasted ten entrance gates, known as pylons. Today, the main entrance to the compound of ruins leads

through an avenue lined with ram-headed sphinxes (below). From there to the Precinct of Mut, more than half a mile away, visitors are faced with one superlative after the other: the tallest obelisk at 30 m (98 ft) weighing 323 tons; the largest columned hall with 134 petrified umbels and papyrus plants, each up to 10 m (33 ft) in circumference; and the largest pylon at 113 m (3,652 ft) wide, 43 m (141 ft) tall and about 15m (49 ft) deep).

In ancient Egypt, a temple was a likeness of the world. Its columns symbolically carried the firmament. The inner sanctum, which even the king could only enter after he had observed strict purification rituals, was hidden in darkness. Main picture: The Great Hypostyle Hall in Karnak.

They are certainly among the more lasting memories of any Nile cruise: The four 20-m-tall (66-ft) colossal statues of King Ramses II (main picture and above). Commissioned by the pharaoh to be hewn straight out of the rock formation on the west bank of the Nile, between the First and the Second Cataract, these giant reliefs are at the gable end of the Great Temple dedicated to Amun-Ra and Re-Harakhte and were completed in the 13th century BC. Behind the entrance to the Great Temple is a hall of columns with giant figures of Ramses II (left). The smaller temple (above) was dedicated to the goddess Hathor and to his wife Nefertari.

When the two giants were in endangered by the future Lake Nasser in the 1960s, UNESCO had them moved 65 m (213 ft) higher up – a massive effort that took four years to complete.

The Great Temple of Ramses II (main picture) would have been submerged in Lake Nasser forever had it not been cut into stone blocks weighing 20 tons each and reassembled at a higher level.

THE NIGER

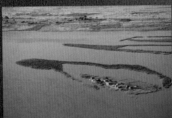

The Niger, Africa's third-largest river, crosses the Sahel and Sahara regions of Mali and Niger on its way from the Guinea Highlands in the south-west to Nigeria. The river has taken the lives of many explorers and travelers, including the Scotsman Mungo Park, but it was not until the mid-19th century that the German geographer Heinrich Barth finally solved the riddle of the river's course. In Mali the Niger turns north in a large arc deep into the desert and then, north of the ancient royal town of Gao, it veers south and finally discharges itself into the sea in Nigeria. The river has always been an important trade route with major posts on both banks.

TIMBUKTU

By 1330, Timbuktu (or Tomboucto) had become one of the most important centers of trade and culture in West Africa. During its heyday in the 15th century, this town on the Niger was the main transshipment center for Saharan trade as well as a focal point for Islamic scholarship. The main points of interest in the northern districts are the medieval university and the Sankoré Mosque (above). It has a pyramid-shaped minaret and is built in traditional mud-brick and wood. It is the model for Islamic buildings in sub-Saharan Africa. The Djinguereber (below) is the oldest mosque and the Sidi Yahya mosque is the smallest.

In the Gao region the Niger runs through barren desert scenery (main picture). Partly navigable during high water, the river ends its journey in a vast delta that covers roughly 25,000 sq km (9,650 sq mi) in the Gulf of Guinea.

Measuring up to 4 m (13 ft) in height and weighing up to 8 tons, the African elephant (main picture, in Amboseli National Park) is the largest living land mammal. An elephant spends fifteen to twenty hours a day feeding and requires 200 to 300 kg (441 to 662 lbs) of food and 100 to 150 liters (22 to 33 gallons) of water.

AMBOSELI

Kenya's most frequented national park owes its popularity to the breathtaking beauty of Mount Kilimanjaro as a backdrop. The relatively small nature reserve, covering an area of only 392 sq km (151 sq mi), boasts an astonishing diversity of species, especially around Lake Amboseli, which attracts large herds with its juicy savannah grass. Black rhino, elephant, buffalo, leopard and lion sightings are often a daily occurrence in Amboseli National Park.

TSAVO

Covering an area of 20,800 sq km (8,029 sq mi), Kenya's largest national park is divided into an eastern and a western part by the parallel road and rail tracks that run through it. While sparse vegetation with thorn bushes and open scrubland predominate in Tsavo East, Tsavo West features denser vegetation. The rolling Taita Hills make the countryside in the west altogether more attractive, but they also make it more difficult to observe the wildlife (above, a leopard).

MASAI MARA

north from the Serengeti. In addition to the interior, which covers roughly 520 sq km (200 sq mi), the Masai Mara Reserve is not reserved for animals alone. The Masai (below), in whose traditional herding and grazing grounds the reserve has been established, are allowed to

The Masai Mara Reserve consists of open, hilly grassland and is situated at an elevation of between 1,500 and 1,700 m (4,922 and 5,578 ft). The Mara and Talek rivers flow through the area year-round, providing an important habitat for hippopotamuses and crocodiles while Burchell's zebra, buffaloes, giraffes and hartebeest graze in the open savannah. From June to October they are joined by some 250,000 Burchell's zebra and 1.3 million wildebeests (above) migrating

continue their semi-nomadic life on the perimeter of the national park. Leopards, cheetahs and the largest population of lions in Kenya are just as much at home here as elephants and a few rare black rhinos. The latter are virtually extinct and now under special protection. The guides in the lodges know the protected area well. It is best to join an organized safari to be sure you see the "big five" (elephants, rhinos, lions, leopards and buffalo) on your trip.

SERENGETI

The Serengeti, a vast savannah east of Lake Victoria, extends from northwestern Tanzania all the way to neighboring Kenya. The "kopjes" (Dutch for "little heads") that rise everywhere from the otherwise flat grasslands (above) are gneiss and quartzite rocks that once lay below the surface of the soil. Laid open by erosion over thousands of years, they now serve as viewpoints for people as well as animals (right, from top to bottom: giraffes, elephants, zebras, lions), but they also provide protection from enemies and the often blazing hot sun. Around 15,000 sq km (5,790 sq mi) of Tanzanian territory have been turned into a national park which is now the setting for an annual mass migration of animals. Each year vast herds of Burchell's zebras, wildebeests and Thomson gazelles trek across the steppe and savannah landscapes of the Serengeti on their quest for water and food, often covering distances up to 1,500 km (932 mi).

NGORONGORO

The Ngorongoro Conservation Area covers 8,000 sq km (3,088 sq mi) of the Ngorongoro crater floor in northern Tanzania. Against the backdrop of an impressive natural landscape (above), thousands of wild animals roam freely, representing a cross-section of the biodiversity here. For a long time this area was part of the Serengeti, which had received its protected status as early as 1921 and was made a national park thirty years later. In 1974 it became an independent wildlife reserve. The floor of the crater, largely covered with grass, is the grazing land for large herds of Masai livestock.

"Siringitu", meaning "endless plain", is the Masai name for the large savannah in northern Tanzania. Twice a year, large herds of graminivores start here on their long migration in search of water and fresh grass, with wildebeests leading the way. Huge herds of Cape buffalo also trek across the Serengeti (main picture).

KILIMANJARO

The Kilimanjaro range rises majestically out of the savannah in northern Tanzania on the border with Kenya (main picture, in the morning light). A national park covering 750 sq km (290 sq mi) has been established here to protect the unique montane forest in the upper regions of the mountain.

Mount Kilimanjaro comprises three main cones and numerous smaller peaks of volcanic origin. In the west is the 4,000-m-high (13,124-ft) Shira; in the middle is Kibo at 5,895 m (19,341 ft), the highest point in Africa; and in the east is the 5,148-m (16,891-ft) Mawenzi. The lesser peaks are lined up along a crevasse that runs from south-east to north-west.

Although it is situated not far from the Equator, the peaks of Kilimanjaro are often covered with snow. The massif in the heart of the savannah features a great range of climate and vegetation zones. Above the savannah is a cultivated agricultural belt and former woodland savannah that today remains only on the northern slopes. This zone blends into the deciduous

montane forest that goes up to 3,000 m (9,843 ft). This is followed by an extensive ericaceous and alpine belt, which itself gives way to the ice-capped summit region. The national park provides a habitat for numerous animals including gazelles, rhinoceroses, Cape buffalo, elephants and leopards, some of them endangered species.

Africa's highest mountain can be climbed during a strenuous five-day trek starting in the Tanzanian village of Marangu. During the ascent, hikers cross into a new vegetation and climate zone every day all the way up to the snow-capped summit of the "Mountain of God" (left).

Victoria Falls are among the most spectacular waterfalls in the world. With ear-shattering force, the Zambezi River, which forms the border between Zambia and Zimbabwe, plunges about 110 m (361 ft) into the abyss, a natural spectacle reflected in the falls' local name: "Mosi-oa-Tunya", or "Smoke that thunders". During the spring floods in March and April, the falls grow into a nearly 2-km-wide (1.2-mi) wide curtain of water with up to 10,000 cu m (353,147 cu ft) of water plummeting over the edge every second. David Livingstone was the first European to see the falls, in 1855, and named them for Queen Victoria of England.

During the rainy season, Victoria Falls, comprising the Devil's Cataract, the Main Falls, Horseshoe Falls, Rainbow Falls and the Eastern Cataract, are considered the largest continuous curtain of water on the planet. Beyond the waterfall, the Zambezi squeezes through the Boiling Pot (above) before overcoming yet more rapids (main picture) and finally pouring itself into Lake Kariba.

Main picture: The deep gorge into which the Zambezi plunges from the crest line of the Victoria Falls was dug out over millions of years. The water continues to erode the soft rock – Victoria Falls are "on the move".

MAKGADIKGADI

Saltpans of all sizes make up the core of the Makgadikgadi. In an area covering about 12,000 sq km (4,362 sq mi) they are not only the largest of their kind in the world but also the most recognizable feature of this part of the Kalahari Desert. Although they appear to be utterly hostile to any form of life, the saltpans are in fact a veritable paradise for certain creatures. Depending on the season, colonies of zebra and herds of antelope settle around their margins (main picture) along with pink flamingos and a number of other animals. During the rains the hard salt crust softens and turns into a treacherous sludge that is impassable for vehicles; the 165-km (103-mi) route across the Makgadikgadi Pan to Kubu Island is only open during the dry season. In the north it rejoins an asphalted road that continues eastward to Nata.

OKAVANGO DELTA

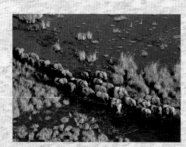

The Okavango Delta in Botswana is a unique natural habitat in the Kalahari Desert. The Okavango River rises in the Angolan highlands and ultimately flows through Namibia and northern Botswana before evaporating and seeping away in this inland delta. Covering a vast area of roughly 15,000 sq km (5,790 sq mi), the delta is a mostly flat terrain with only few high spots. It floods each year in June (above) when the waters of the Cuando River arrive after the rainy season.

CHOBE

Chobe National Park, which has existed in its present size since 1968, covers about 12,000 sq km (4,362 sq mi) of widely differing ecosystems ranging from the Chobe riverfront, which features dense vegetation, to open woodland savannah and barren desert-like terrain. Chobe's great treasures are its elephant herds and prides of lions (above). Aside from the banks of the Chobe River, the Savuti Marshes in the south-west of the park also offer a rich variety of wildlife and habitats.

"Etosha" means "Great white place" and refers to the vast saltpans in Etosha National Park that provide sanctuary for the numerous animal species here. Elephants, which were nearly extinct in the area, have been able to reproduce here in great numbers, and the parl's population of black and white rhinoceroses is one of the largest in Africa. Cheetahs, lions, leop- ards, hyenas, bat-eared foxes and jack- als find a gluttonous menu including vast herds of antelopes, gazelles, zebras and giraffes. Right: A Kudu calf falls prey to a lioness. The birds are similarly fascinating, ranging from bizarre marabou storks to yellow- beaked tokos. Flamingos even arrive after the rains. Visitors can enjoy the spectacle from safe viewing areas.

Visitors at Etosha National Park can choose from three rest areas to view the incredible animal kingdom here, but only between sunrise and sunset. Main picture: Gazelles and zebras in a moment of leisure.

"Nature is relentless and unchangeable, and she is indifferent as to whether her hidden motivations and actions are understandable to humans or not" – Galileo Galilei. Left: Lions resting after a feed.

The main attraction of Namib Naukluft National Park is the Sossusvlei (main picture), home to a sensual dune landscape that stretches in gloriously shaped waves as far as the eye can see.

NAMIB NAUKLUFT

Covering a vast area of 50,000 sq km (19,300 sq mi), Namib Naukluft National Park is one of the largest nature reserves in the world. It comprises the Naukluft Range and a large portion of the Namib Desert, which goes straight down to the coast and is about 1,500 km (932 mi) long and 80 to 130 km (50 to 81 mi) wide. Although the area is nothing but subtropical desert landscape, it nevertheless boasts great species diversity. The geological features range from blackish gravel plains and regions of strangely eroded island mountains to dune seas in the Central Namib. The Naukluft Range has rugged peaks that reach nearly 2,000 m (6,562 ft) and dramatic valleys that together form a unique ecosystem. First and foremost, there is sufficient water here to provide for a diverse range of flora and fauna while mountain zebra, baboons, jackals and springboks coexist with a number of bird species including Nubian vultures, dune larks and Gray's larks. The latter two are indigenous to these gravel plains.

SOSSUSVLEI

The desert is alive – tracks on the mighty sand dunes of the Sossusvlei testify to the nighttime activities in what at first glance seems a totally inhospitable environment. Some of these small desert-dwellers include darkling beetles and some scorpion varieties, but even larger gerbils, jackals and Oryx antelopes – their bodies perfectly adapted to the arid climate – also manage to find sufficient food here. And when the rains are good, the Tsauchab River carries plenty of water in from the highlands and will even flood the so-called *vlei*, the depressions in the dunes.

KOKERBOOM FOREST

Quiver trees, part of the Aloe family, were given their name by the San, a Namibian people of hunters and gatherers who used its hollow branches as quivers for their arrows. The unassuming plant prefers a rocky ground and usually grows as a solitary tree making the forest of quiver trees growing near Keetmanshop in southern Namibia a rather unusual sight.

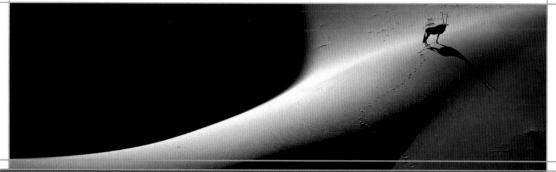

The Oryx antelope carefully takes up a scent (left). What it can smell is the humid air from the Atlantic whose precious moisture the animal needs in order to survive. To do so, it stands on the crest of a dune waiting for the mist banks to drift inland, then it licks the drops of water that condense on its nostrils.

FISH RIVER CANYON

With a length of 161 km (100 mi) and a depth of 450 to 550 m (1,476 to 1,805 ft), this is the second largest gorge in the world after the Grand Canyon. From above it is easy to make out the two different levels of the canyon. The first canyon, on a north-south axis, is a rift valley about 20 km (12 mi) wide that was created by tectonic shifting in the plateau during the Paleozoic about 500 million years ago. During an ice age some 200 million years later, the glaciers further deepened this valley. For the last 50 million years or so, since the Tertiary, the Fish River has carved its course into the canyon, further eroding it over time and in the process creating the second portion of the

Fish River Canyon in southern Namibia is the largest gorge in Africa.

canyon, which is also the narrowest and deepest section. From the vista point, a steep path takes visitors down to the valley floor. Hiking the Fish River Canyon is a challenge, however. The trail leads from Hikers' View to the Ai-Ais Hot Springs resort about 85 km (53 mi) away at the southern exit from the canyon. The trek lasts a good four days and takes you across the more or less dry riverbed several times. It passes the German Soldiers' Grave (the officers died during a skirmish between German soldiers and the South-West African Nama in 1905). Encounters with baboons, Hartmann's mountain zebras and klip-springers are not uncommon. The glorious conclusion to the hike, which is only permitted during the cool time of year, are the hot springs of Ai-Ais. The name comes from the Nama language and means "hot water" – the thermal springs have a surface temperature of 60 °C (140 °F).

TABLE MOUNTAIN, CAPE TOWN

For a long time the area around Cape Town's working port seemed to have been left to decay. At the end of the 1980s, however, following the model of Fisherman's Wharf in San Francisco, the elegant shopping and entertainment district of Victoria & Alfred Waterfront was created. The yachts and the fishing boats in the harbor add to the charm of the area (main picture).

TABLE MOUNTAIN

The Khoikhoï people native to the region called Table Mountain (right) "Hoeri 'kwaggo", meaning "sea mountain". It owes its present name to the first European man to ascend the mountain, the Portuguese Antonio da Saldanha, who christened it Taboa do Cabo, or Table of the Cape, in 1503.

Today no one has to climb Table Mountain on foot anymore: the tramway takes visitors from the valley station right to the top. Other peaks around Table Mountain and Cape Town include Lion's Head and Signal Hill in the north-west and the Twelve Apostles to the south-west.

CAPE TOWN

Framed in by Table Mountain and its auxiliary peaks (below: Lion's Head) on one side and the ocean on the other, Cape Town's historical and multicultural essence is plainly evidenced in the former colonial buildings on Long Street and the variety of people who have settled here. It is also considered one of the most attractive urban centers in the world. Since it was founded in 1652 by Jan van Riebeeck, the city has steadily increased in size and now has roughly 3.5 million people.

The Castle of Good Hope, built in around 1679 in the star fort style, reflects colonial history in its Victorian and Cape Dutch architecture. Former suburbs like Bo Kaap now have a distinctly Asian flair to them. The main attraction for night owls is the Victoria & Alfred Waterfront. Here, water lovers can choose between the beaches on the Atlantic side of the Cape peninsula and those in False Bay, which – although still on the Atlantic side, not the Indian Ocean side – is not affected by the cold waters of the Benguela current. This current originates in the Antarctic and cools the waters on South Africa's west coast to a chilly 12 to 15 °C (54 to 59 °F), while in False Bay the sea can reach a pleasantly warm 20 °C (68 °F) on hot summer days. Left: The traditional seaside resort of Muizenberg.

South Africa boasts one-tenth of all the flowering plant species in the world – more than all European countries put together! The most spectacular of all is the Giant or King Protea, South Africa's incredibly hardy, gloriously colorful national flower (main picture).

WINELANDS

Jan van Riebeeck, founder of Cape Town, was clever enough to order grapevines for his trading post and in 1654 tasted the first drops of locally produced Muscadet wine. The royal courts of Europe appreciated the South African libation at the time, but Cape wines did not really come into their own until the beginning of the 1990s, when the international trade embargo was lifted. South African vintners then began creating top wines, some in cooperation with renowned European vineyards. The idyllic wine-growing region northeast of Cape Town, which has a very European look about it, quickly became a popular travel destination.

GARDEN ROUTE

South Africa's most famous road, the Garden Route, runs for about 200 km (124 mi) from Mossel Bay to Storm River along the Indian Ocean coastline with its many charming bays and coves. Among the best-known sights along the way is Knysna Lagoon, which is best viewed from the rocky cliffs of Knysna Head. Knysna Forest nearby is South Africa's largest woodland, home to yellowwood

Mossel Bay (top) marks the beginning of the Garden Route with its abundant wildflowers (middle). The Outeniqua Choo-Tjoe Train (bottom) takes visitors up and down the coast.

trees that can grow to be 800 years old. It is also a haven for the nearly extinct African forest elephants. Plettenberg Bay is probably the most popular beach resort on the Garden Route, where upscale hotels and elegant beach villas belonging to wealthy South Africans line the powdery white beaches. During the winter months, whales come into the bay to calve. A section of the coast here is covered in dense primeval forest and protected within Tsitsikamma National Park.

The first vines were planted in South Africa in the 17th century. Vineyards such as Boschendal (opposite page) now enjoy worldwide recognition. Groot Constantia (far left) is South Africa's oldest vineyard. The Kooperatiewe Wijnbouwers Vereeniging is in Paarl. Left and center: Lanzerac Manor and Winery near Stellenbosch.

Madagascar's appeal lies in its exceptional world of flora and fauna, dazzling coral reefs, bizarre limestone formations, volcanic craters, endless sandy beaches and the relics of ancient civilizations. The island is tropical, with the exception of its very southern tip. Its length of 1,580 km (982 mi), means that the climate and vegetation zones differ greatly between the north and the south. The backbone of the landscape is formed by mountain ranges and volcanoes that run nearly the entire length of the island. The eastern highlands drop steeply down to the Indian Ocean coast while in the west they drop off into the coastal lowlands along the Mozambique Channel. The west coast is much drier and more fragmented with coves and promontories than the east coast and is dominated by a savannah landscape that features impressive, towering baobab trees (bottom left). Influenced by the south-easterly trade winds, the east side of Madagascar is covered with lush rainforest. In addition, there are a number of islands off Madagascar's nearly 5,000-km (3,107-mi) coast which, like Nosy Be in the north-west and Nosy Sainte-Marie in the east, for instance, are surrounded by coral reefs that make them prized swimming and diving territory.

Insets, clockwise from the top left: Lemurs on the razor-sharp rock needles in the Ankarana Reserve; the canyon systems; spectacular cliff formations of the Isalo Mountains; the peaks of the Andringitra National Park reflected in a lake; Baobab Alley, not far from Morondava; and the dramatic limestone landscape of Tsingy de Bemaraha National Park.

The world's fourth-largest island split off from the African continent about 130 million years ago. Its flora and fauna – today protected by several national parks – therefore developed completely independently ever since. There are now thirty-eight different species of chameleon on Madagascar, for example (main picture).

SEYCHELLES

The Seychelles are a tropical island paradise. The rocky Anse Soleil beach is on the main island of Mahé (main picture) whose urban center, Victoria, is often referred to as the smallest capital in the world.

This group of islands, "discovered" in the western Indian Ocean by Vasco da Gama in 1501, comprises more than one hundred individual islands, fewer than half of which are actually inhabited. While many of the islands are no more than coral reefs or atolls (covering a total surface area of about 210 sq km/81 sq mi), the main islands of Mahé, Praslin, Silhouette and La Digue are quite mountainous with the peaks on Mahé, the largest island at 158 sq km (61 sq mi), reaching an altitude of up to 905 m (2,969 ft) and featuring only very sparse vegetation. The tropical oceanic climate means that the year is divided into a dry, and relatively cool, season (from May to September) and a hot, rainy north-west monsoon season (from December to March). As far as religion is concerned, a large majority of the population is Roman Catholic. The ethnic breakdown is mixed including Asian, African and European (mainly French). The brisk tourist trade means that residents of the Seychelles have the highest per capita income of all African countries; about ninety percent of them live on Mahé.

Located about 6 km (4 mi) east of Praslin, the Seychelles island of La Digue is characterized by giant, smooth granite blocks that owe their pale red hue to embedded feldspar (left).

Discovered by the Portuguese mariner
Pedro de Mascarenhas in about 1510, the
island of Mauritius (main picture: Tamarin
Bay) belongs to the group of islands
called the Mascarene Islands, which are
named after him and which include the
now French island of Réunion.

The small islands of Mauritius and Réunion belong to the Mascarene Islands, a group of islands around 850 km (528 mi) east of Madagascar. The first European to discover the islands was a Portuguese mariner named Pedro Mascarenhas at the beginning of the 16th century. Both islands were formed by a hotspot in the earth's crust – at eight million years old Mauritius is the oldest island in the group while Réunion is only three million years old.

Réunion's mountainous landscape is dominated by the 3,070-m (10,073-ft) Piton de Neiges, with its wild yet dormant calderas (cirques), while its smaller neighbor, the 2,632-m (8,636-ft) Piton de la Fournaise (right), is one of the most active volcanoes in the world. A lovely trail to the Trois Bassins of St-Gilles-les-Hautes on the west coast of the island leads to the Bassin des Aigrettes, where several waterfalls cascade over the cliffs (below).

A ring of coral reefs has formed in the warm tropical waters of the Indian Ocean around the volcanic heart of Mauritius, producing ideal conditions for a rich underwater world. On land the original tropical vegetation is now only found in a few places in the south-west while most of the island, which otherwise features just a few imposing mountains (far left: the Trois Mamelles), is taken up with sugar cane fields.

The Golden Gate and the sparkling San Francisco skyline, the red sandstone towers of Monument Valley, the grandiose gorges of the Grand Canyon, the endless expanse of the prairie, the legacy of the Aztecs and Mayans, baroque pomp at the Popocatépetl, Highway 1 and Route 66, New York…from the green jungles of the Amazon and the ice caps of the world's highest volcano to the immense glaciers of Patagonia, the mysterious ruins of the Incas and the colonial heritage of the Europeans…the list seems never-ending. Welcome to the Americas!

VANCOUVER

Vancouver is simply one of the loveliest cities in the world. Superbly situated on the idyllic northern Pacific Coast and surrounded by picturesque bays and the majestic mountains of the nearby Coast Range, this modern metropolis also has its share of glass skyscrapers, a quaint Old Town, spacious Stanley Park, sandy beaches, the Lion's Gate Bridge, as well as the futuristic Canada Place. Few cities harmonize so comfortably with the invit-

ing wilderness nearby. Granville Island is an artificial leisure island under the highway bridges out on False Creek. The converted warehouses here were reassigned as restaurants, bars and shops, with artists and craftspeople working in their galleries. The past still shines brightly in Gastown while vibrant, exotic restaurants and shops are the focus in Chinatown. Vancouver is also a city of immigrants who do well to celebrate their cultures.

VANCOUVER ISLAND

Vancouver Island is a true paradise for the people of greater Vancouver – an island with a stunning natural environment totally separated from the urban bustle nearby, and yet in such close proximity to all of the comforts of the city. Victoria (right), the capital of Vancouver Island, is a former Hudson Bay Company trading fort.

Main picture: Cruise ships and Asian cargo ships are the main features of Vancouver Harbor, an important commercial hub that maintains a brisk trade across the Pacific.

Main picture: Water crashes down with a deafening roar over Horseshoe Falls, the Canadian side of Niagara Falls (*Niagara* is a Native American term meaning "thundering water").

TORONTO

Toronto is a surprisingly lively city. Ambitious construction projects indicate dynamic development, while traditional buildings such as Holy Trinity Church, a Catholic church from the 19th century, are protected heritage sites. Particularly worth seeing are Ontario Place, a futuristic leisure and shopping area on Lake Ontario that hosts rotating exhibitions, and the Harbourfront Centre, a contemporary arts and cultural center in converted warehouses located on the piers with shops, restaurants, waterfront cafés, art galleries and theaters as well as the Queen's Quay and York Quay Promenades. Toronto Islands, linked with the city by ferry, is a tranquil sanctuary featuring quiet canals, gentle strolls and a historic amusement park for children. The CN Tower is the city's emblem and is visible from vast distances. The viewing platform offers superb views over the city and its surroundings. Other highlights include the BCE Place, a bold skyscraper with a light-flooded atrium and Yorkville, Toronto's "Greenwich Village".

NIAGARA FALLS

Niagara Falls – a very popular travel destination for honeymooners – are located on the short but powerful Niagara River, which flows north from Lake Erie into Lake Ontario in Canada. The border between the USA and Canada runs through the middle of the falls.

Known for centuries by Native Americans as Thundering Water, the first white man to see Niagara was a Jesuit priest by the name of Louis Hennepin, who came in December 1678. The huge volume of water drops more than 50 m (164 ft) over the escarpment in a massive cloud

Niagara Falls are on the border between the USA and Canada, and are split by tiny Goat Island. The falls produce an average of 4,200 cu m (150,000 cu ft) of water per second.

of mist and spray. The river is actually split into two channels by tiny Goat Island: the large Horseshoe Falls are on the Canadian side and the smaller American Falls are on the U.S. side. Rainbow Bridge links the two countries. Table Rock to the west, next to the horseshoe-shaped falls, or the Minolta Tower, are recommended as observation points. The best view is afforded by the "Maid of the Mist" which sails right past the falls. The more adventurous visitor will take a "Journey Behind the Falls", a particularly impressive and unforgettable experience.

Rising boldly above the Toronto skyline, the CN Tower (left) at 555.3 m (1815 ft) was the tallest free-standing structure in the world for thirty-one years (Burj Dubai now holds that title). CN stands for Canadian National, the railway company responsible for its construction, which only took 40 months.

MONTREAL

Montreal (above, with the market hall dome towering over the Old Town) was founded by French Catholics in 1642. Today, seventy-five percent of the city's residents can still claim French ancestry.

Situated at the confluence of the St Lawrence and Ottawa Rivers, Montreal quickly grew into a prosperous center of trade. The French influence remains strong in Vieux-Montreal, the lovely Old Town featuring a good number of historical buildings and narrow streets on the southern slopes of Mont Royal, while an air of urban life prevails in the inner city.

After Paris, Montreal is the second-largest city in the world where French is spoken. In the winter, residents take refuge in the underground city – "la ville souterraine" – with its network of tunnels, passageways and shopping malls. The Basilique Notre-Dame, a splendid Catholic church (below), was built by prominent Protestant architect James O'Donnell.

City lights: A view of the glittering city from Montreal's 223-m-high (732-ft) Mont-Royal.

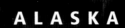

KOBUK VALLEY

GATES OF THE ARCTIC

DENALI

The valleys of the Kobuk River recall the days when ancestors of the Inuits and Native Americans arrived in Alaska via the land-bridge from Siberia. Scientists believe it was some 12,000 years ago that they migrated to North America, when the same vegetation grew in the Kobuk Valley as today in the tundra, but at the time it had not yet been flooded by the ocean separating the two continents. Founded in 1980, this national park features astonishing sand dunes that rise up to 30 m (98 ft) high and extend across an area of 40 sq km (15 sq mi). Especially worth seeing here is a place known as Onion Portage, where giant herds of caribou (above) have arrived via this ford for thousands of years – only to be awaited by hunters on the shores. Countless weapons and tools have been excavated from the early encampments here that span a period of nearly 10,000 years.

In northern Alaska, two particularly striking peaks rise up like silent guardians from the Brooks Range to form a natural barrier between the valleys of the south and the seeminlgy endless plains of the north. Robert Marshall, a scientist and explorer who lived on the Koyukuk River as well as in North Fork between 1929 and 1939, named them the peaks "Frigid Crags" and "Boreal", but they are better known as the "Gates of the Arctic", also the name of the national park that was founded here in 1980 and extends to the north beyond the giant mountains. It is a vast area of mountains, rivers, lakes and wholly untamed nature, home to only a few Inuit. At the Anaktuvuk Pass the Inuit even established a small settlement in order to wait for the annual migration of the giant caribou herds there. The national park is four times the size of Yellowstone.

Mount McKinley and the surrounding glaciers, forests and lakes were all placed under protection back in 1917. In those days only a few adventurers were able to enjoy the beauty of the park, but when the Denali Highway was completed in 1957, ordinary folks could also discover the glory of the highest peak in the USA. Denali National Park offers nature in its unadulterated state, having remained virtually unchanged despite tourism. It owes its almost paradisiacal state mainly to the fact that private vehicles are not allowed to enter the area.

WRANGELL-ST. ELIAS   GLACIER BAY

The American bald eagle has been the national bird of the United States since 1782. These majestic creatures live mainly in Alaska and their wingspans of up to 2.4 m (8 ft) make them one of the most impressive birds in the world.

Wrangell-St Elias is the largest national park in the United States and is also home to the country's second-highest peak after Mount McKinley (6,194 m/20,323 ft): Mount St Elias, at 5,489 m (18,009 ft). More than one hundred glaciers here form the largest ice field south of the Arctic Circle. The Wrangell-St Elias wilderness area is the largest of its kind in the States and features impressive gorges and raging torrents where few traces of human existence can be seen except in the two copper towns of McCarthy and Kenicott. It became a national park in 1980.

"And here, too, one learns that the world, though made, is yet being made; that this is still the morning of creation; that mountains long conceived are now being born; that moraine soil is being ground and outspread for coming plants; to make the mountains and valleys and plains of other predestined landscapes, to be followed by still others in endless rhythm and beauty" – John Muir, October 1879. Little needs to be added. Nowhere else can you observe the constant transformation of nature as easily and as intimately as in Glacier National Park.

Main picture: The tall art deco towers of the Golden Gate Bridge, which are visible from almost any high point in the city, are two of the most recognizable icons of West Coast. When the structure was completed in 1937 it was the longest suspension bridge in the world.

SAN FRANCISCO

attractions are the Golden Gate Bridge, Fisherman's Wharf, the marina at the end of Hyde Street, Chinatown with its restaurants and shops, the Victorian houses on Alamo Square, the bustle of Market Street, trendy districts such as South of Market and of course a ride on the cable car (below).

The "City on the seven hills" (there are officially 43 hills) is regarded as one of the most attractive metropolises in the world. Founded in 1776 by Spanish explorers and originally called Yerba Buena, it received its present name in 1847, after Mission San Francisco de Asis founded by Father Junipero Serra. The first gold discoveries in January 1848 brought on the rise of the city as an important trading center and seaport. Even the catastrophic earthquake of 1906 could not slow the boom. Among its main

THE REDWOODS

Three nature reserves in northern California – Jedediah Smith, Del Norte Coast and Prairie Creek – owe their existence to a nature conservation movement focused primarily on saving the redwoods. Together with Redwood National Park (above), which is home to the great horned owl, North America's largest long-eared owl, they form a unified reserve. Redwoods, close relatives of the sequoias, reach heights of more than 100 m (328 ft) and live an average of 500 to 700 years with some reaching more than 2,000 years of age. The

tallest trees are in the Tall Trees Grove near Orick. Prairie Creek is home to a dense rainforest, and the Del Norte Coast has a rugged coastline. Giant redwoods can also be seen on Mill Creek in Redwoods State Park and on the superb Avenue of the Giants.

The Merced River has dug itself deeply into the primeval landscape of this glorious park and formed a deep, elongated valley, at the bottom of which are the visitor center and some lodges. Yosemite Valley is dominated by two giant rock faces: Half Dome (above) and El Capitan. The latter, at 2,307 m (7,590 ft), is an absolute mecca among rock climbers, its 910 m (3,100 ft) face presenting one of the most dramatic challenges in the world for that sport. The magnificent Half Dome rises to 2,695 m (7,569 ft) from the valley floor and looks as if its other half simply broke off. This rock was formed around 250,000 years ago by powerful masses of ice at a time when humans did not yet roam the continent and when Glacier Point, today one of the most attractive viewpoints in the American West some 100 m (328 ft) above the valley, was still hidden under a thick layer of ice. In fact, the first humans first arrived in Yosemite Valley back in the Ice Age. They would have even experienced Tenaya Lake when it was still a glacier. Powerful natural forces did indeed shape this valley, giving form to the granite, but that process is still not complete. Yosemite Falls and Bridal Veil Falls are still at work on the valley floor and walls.

Yosemite National Park (main picture with El Capitan lit by the evening sun and the Merced River in the foreground) is one of the oldest national parks in the United States. The first areas were declared nature reserves as early as the 1860s and in 1905 it reached its present size. Many of the main attractions are situated in the roughly 10-km-long (6-mi) Yosemite Valley, in the heart of the park. Must-sees include the impressive peaks such as El Capitan or Half Dome as well as the Yosemite Falls (left), which plunge 739 m (2,425 ft) down the rock face.

LAS VEGAS

Las Vegas, the glittering gambling metropolis in the Nevada desert, has fascinated visitors since the 1940s with its casinos and flashing neon lights. In those days, Bugsy Siegel, an infamous underworld boss from the East Coast, opened the first gambling palace in this otherwise desolate expanse: the Flamingo Hotel. Gambling was legalized in Las Vegas as early as 1931. Casino after casino began popping, and Bugsy Siegel became ever richer from his (almost) honest work. The city comes alive in the evening when the bright neon signs flicker along the Strip, the famous entertainment boulevard

in Las Vegas, and the gambling-happy tourists are brought in by the busload. It was not until the 1990s that Las Vegas transformed itself into a giant theme park. As gambling is prohibited to anyone under the age of 21, "entertainment for the entire family" has become a priority to draw adults.

Main picture: Vast hotels like the Luxor (modeled after pyramids of Egypt) and the New York, New York, are palaces of entertainment sometimes featuring rollercoasters and special effects in their lobbies – and of course giant casinos. Only one thing seems to be missing: clocks. Vegas is always open!

YELLOWSTONE

It is the microorganisms in the Grand Prismatic Spring in Yellowstone National Park that give the soil and water their vivid colors (main picture). Opposite page from top: A fascinating diversity of landscapes, set away from the paved roads.

Explorer and trapper John Colter was the first white man to ever see the area that is now Yellowstone. He told of hot springs shooting out of the ground, of bison and bears, and praised the area as one of the great paradises of the American West. Indeed, the earth below the park is in an ongoing state of upheaval here. The Grand Canyon of Yellowstone and the bubbling geysers here remind us of ancient volcanic eruptions, and there are more than 300 hot springs within the park. Cold filters its way down into hot chambers nearly 2 km (1.2 mi) below the surface where it is then heated and expelled again through narrow channels as a mixture of steam and water. Official catwalks take visitors through the misty landscape where geysers constantly emit foul-smelling sulfurous smoke.

The idea to transform the area into a national park originally came from the members of the Washburn-Langford-Doane expedition, which began its exploration of the region as early as 1870. Finally, in 1872, Yellowstone was declared the first national park of the United States.

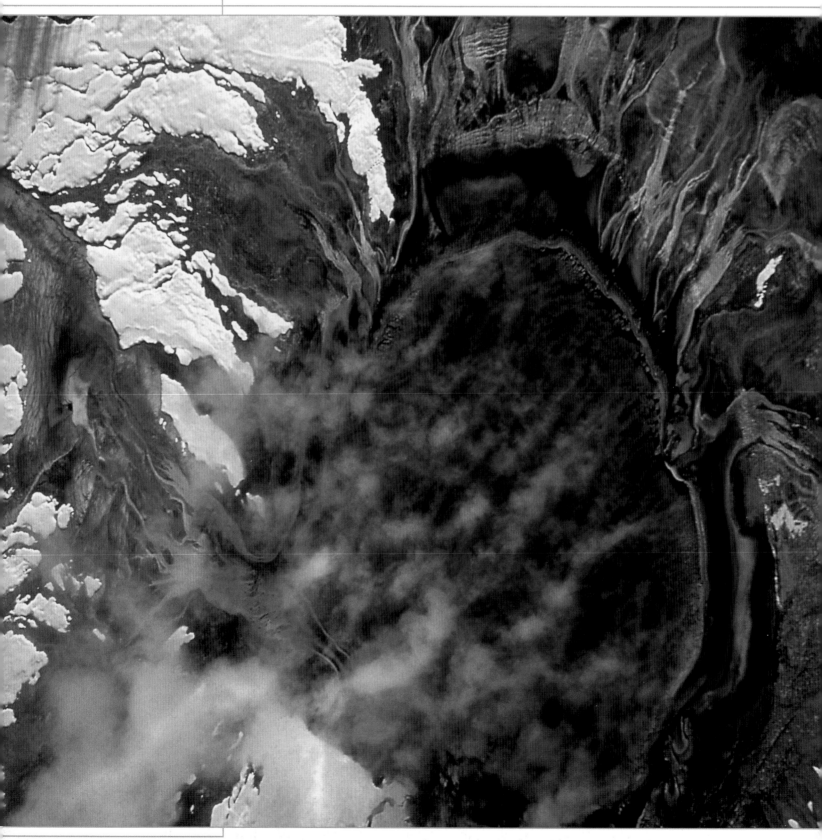

The oldest national park in the United States is a majestic wilderness of mountains, rivers, lakes and more than 300 geysers. Left: The hot waters of the White Dome Geyser are heated underground and then erupt in a giant plume.

BRYCE CANYON

ZION

The red rock towers of Bryce Canyon rise like organ pipes from the stony ground. These colorful limestone formations, eroded by wind and weather over the course of millions of years, boast imaginative names such as Thor's Hammer, Queen's Castle, Gulliver's Castle, Hindu Temples and Wall Street. Nowhere else has nature been this capricious, not even in the Grand Canyon.

John Wesley Powell was the first white man to explore the Canyon in about 1870. The national park owes its name to Ebenezer Bryce, who built a farm in Bryce Canyon but soon moved on to Arizona. Apparently, the arduous task of spending weeks on end trying to find his cattle in the nooks and crannies here finally got to him. Bryce Canyon has been a national park since 1924. Native Americans have a more interesting name for the area: "red rocks standing like men in a bowl-shaped canyon".

Zion National Park in southern Utah features breathtaking high plateaus, deep gorges and massive plateaus. Over the millennia, the Virgin River has carved its way into the colorful stone, forming Zion Canyon, which was given its Biblical name by the Mormons, who were the first to settle in the area. They had been searching for fertile farming country and believed they had found Heaven on Earth. They named the impressive rock formations after the Bible too, using names such as East and West Temple or Great White Throne. Zion became a national park in 1919. A paved road takes you through the canyon along the Virgin River, a tributary of the Colorado River, up to the Temple of Sinawava, 13 km (8 mi) away. From there, a hiking trail takes visitors to Weeping Rock, a mossy overhanging rock, as well as to Angel's Landing, a striking chunk of mountain.

Main picture: Bryce canyon with its organ pipes made from stone. Other attractions include Bryce Amphitheater.

MONUMENT VALLEY

Arguably one of the most beautiful valleys in the world, Monument Valley on the Utah-Arizona border is on that list of "eighth wonders". It is indeed a magical world of red rock formations and perhaps the most recognizable symbol of the classic American Southwest. The countless films that have been shot here have transformed it into a near-mythical landscape. Harry Goulding, the owner of a trading post here, was the first to introduce John Ford – the director of such film classics as "Fort Apache", "The Searchers" and "Stagecoach" – to this impressive natural set, where colossal sandstone towers and stony spires rise out of the desert into the sky like monuments to the gods themselves. They boast fanciful names such as "Left Glove" and "Right Glove"; one slim rocky needle is known as "Totem Pole", while three rock needles standing in a line, once known as the "Three Sisters", have been renamed as "Big W" for John Wayne, who shot so many films here. They form a giant W when silhouetted against the sky. The valley is only accessible via a 22-km-long (14-mi) circuit route while the onward journey is only possible with a Navajo tour guide. The money is a donation to tribal coffers.

Main picture: Monument Valley south of
Moab, Utah, has become famous through
John Ford's many western films. The
Navajo Indians' Tribal Park there was
made a conservation area in 1960.

The Colorado River meanders its way for 446 km (277 mi) through this breathtakingly beautiful system of gorges that are between 5.5 and 30 km (3.5 and 19 miles) wide and up to 1,800 m (5,906 ft) deep (main picture).

In 1540, the Spaniard López de Cárdenas was the first European to see the magnificent panorama of the Grand Canyon, but it took until the middle of the 19th century before the vast area was accurately mapped.

The origins of the Grand Canyon are still not entirely clear. Presumably, the Colorado River began to carve a path through the rocky plateau around six million years ago and, over the course of time, the gorge grew. John Muir, an influential and passionate naturalist, called it the "grandest of God's terrestrial cities". Wind and weather obviously contributed to the shaping of rock cliffs and bizarre rock formations, and the sequence of sedimentary layers in the stone documents the various geological periods. Fossils that were found in the canyon provide important information on life in primeval times. Temperatures in the canyon can rise to 50 °C (122 °F), but only a few exceptionally resilient plants and animals are capable of withstanding this heat including some species of cacti and thorn bushes. Rattlesnakes, black widow spiders and scorpions also call it home.

CHICAGO

The metropolis on Lake Michigan (main picture) is the third-largest city in the United States. After the 2008 presidential elections, the city was renamed "Obama City". Barack Obama began his political career here before making it to the White House.

SKYLINE

Chicago was already an important transport and trading hub in the state of Illinois back in the 19th century. During the "Roaring 1920s", Al Capone's "Windy City" gained a deservedly dubious reputation as a metropolis of gangsters. For two days in October of 1871, a devastating fire destroyed almost the entire city. From among the many old buildings, only the historic Water Tower still stands today. The new Chicago was built on top of the charred ruins of the former city, and proved a perfect chance to show the enterprising spirit of the inhabitants. Aside from New York, no other city in the United States has a more impressive skyline than Chicago.

THE LOOP

The Loop, an area of downtown Chicago encircled by the "L" (elevated mass transit railway), is bordered by the Chicago River in the north and the west, Michigan Avenue in the east and Roosevelt Avenue in the south. It is basically the heart of this fascinating metropolis. State Street, the largest pedestrian zone in the world, lures visitors with its department stores, boutiques, restaurants, cinemas

Traffic rarely stops inside the Loop (top) even at night. Bottom: LaSalle Street Station.

and theaters. Even the sidewalk is full of surprises, among them the City of Chicago Public Art Program's 16-m-high (53-ft) untitled sculpture by Pablo Picasso at the Richard J. Daley Civic Center Plaza; the "Flamingo, Alexander Calder's giant spider in front of the Chicago Federal Center;, the "Universe", a giant mobile by the same artist that hangs in the lobby of the Sears Tower; and "The Four Seasons", a 20-m-long (66-ft) mosaic wall by Marc Chagall in what is now the Chase Tower Plaza.

Chicago became a virtual El Dorado for architects after the great fire of 1871, which almost completely destroyed the city, and they still seem to have more freedom here than in New York or San Francisco, for example. Left: A modern office block downtown. Opposite page: Chicago Tribune Tower.

CHICAGO BLUES

Gifted artists such as Muddy Waters, Howlin' Wolf, Elmore James and Little Walter all left a permanent mark on the Chicago Blues and their music is still popular today. As a genre, it forms part of the soundtrack for a journey through African American history, when the blues developed as an independent style from popular traditional songs. Like the rock 'n' roll of the 1950s, the Chicago Blues also emerged from the Mississippi Delta Blues of the South.

Murals on the south side (top) recall the early days of Chicago blues. Bottom: A still life with bass drum and trumpet case in Blue Chicago.

Before World War II, Chicago already boasted a lively music scene firmly rooted in Glenn Miller's big band swing sound, but it was less rootsy than the Chicago blues that would soon develop. Muddy Waters brought his version of the "dirty" blues from Clarksdale, spicing it up with a bit of electric guitar. Later blues greats including John Lee Hooker from nearby Detroit and Howlin' Wolf from Memphis, Tennessee, followed in his footsteps, helping to create a sound that greatly influenced a number of styles including rhythm and blues, country, rock 'n' roll and jazz, a genre that is unthinkable without the "blue notes", or worried notes. Jazz and blues still characterize the sound of the city in Chicago today.

NEW YORK CITY

New York, New York – so much more than a mere city, the Big Apple is both a symbol and a likeness of the American Dream itself. For some it is a place to be in the middle of it all, for others it may be a Babylon to avoid if at all possible. Whatever your preference, however, New York does have something for everyone It's loud and hectic and overwhelming at times, but it is a multicultural Eden that is capable of reinventing itself every single day.

"The town presented itself as gigantic, confusing, unfathomable and beautiful ... with blinding rows of windows and dark urban canyons," Jack Kerouac once wrote about New York Main picture: The concrete canyons of Manhattan.

MIAMI, MIAMI BEACH

The MacArthur Causeway was opened in 1997 and forms an almost 2.5-km-long (1.5-mi) link between the southern tip of Miami Beach and the mainland (right). It takes just a few minutes to get from the office towers to the beach – and this is what life in Miami is all about: the beach. The city (above: a hip-hop party; far right: a "sexy body contest") is avant-garde and progressive as well as being a gateway to the Spanish-speaking world of the Caribbean and South America. The Latin American influence gives it a vibrant and cosmopolitan feel and more than 50 percent of the population speaks Spanish – even higher than cities like Denver or San Diego.

Out on Key Biscayne, Miami turns tropical. The island was christened the "Little South Seas" in the old days because it served as the backdrop for Hollywood films meant to be set in Hawaii and Tahiti. From Biscayne Bay, visitors get a fascinating view of the skyline of Downtown Miami (above). Coconut Grove, with its elegant boutiques and southern street cafés, is the place to see and be seen. In the evening, the most popular spot is South Beach, the southernmost section of Miami Beach. This narrow spit of land was derided as "God's waiting room" until the 1980s, because it was a favorite retirement area for impoverished pensioners. Then came the cult TV series "Miami Vice", and the sad nursing homes transformed into "Miami Nice". The pastel-shaded Art Deco hotels on Ocean Drive were given a facelift, and wealthy entrepreneurs turned on the style.

The Florida Keys – small islands in the far southern reaches of the state (above) – wouldn't even be marked on the map had it not been for businessman Henry Flagler's ingenious idea to link them via bridges, thus incorporating them into Florida as the "American Caribbean". Initially, a railroad linked Miami and Key West, but a hurricane tore it away. It was then replaced by the "Overseas Highway", a 200-km-long (130-mi) bridge that carries US Route 1 through all of the keys. Key West, once known as a tropical paradise and hangout, has since become a busy resort with a distinctly Caribbean ambience. Author Ernest Hemingway lived there in a house on Whitehead Street that has since been turned into a museum and opened to the public (below).

THE EVERGLADES

The Everglades offer an ideal for a number of endangered species including aquatic birds like the snowy egret and sea-dwelling mammals such as the West Indian manatee, or sea cow. The Mississippi alligator, which grows up to 6 m (20 ft) in length, is also at home here (main pictures, from left to right).

Mangrove woods and marshes overgrown with sawgrass form a unique ecosystem in southern Florida and offer a perfect habitat for a fascinating range of animal and plant life. The Everglades cover an overall area of 5,661 sq km (2,185 sq mi) that extends from the Tamiami Trail in the north to Florida Bay in the south, and from the Florida Keys in the east to the Gulf of Mexico in the west. A national park since 1947, Native Americans originally referred to the area as "pay-hay-okee", meaning the "sea of grass".

The low altitude and lack of natural drainage have caused the region's high precipitation to collect here, which ultimately formed a vast network of swamps. Unfortunately, the complex ecosystem of the Everglades is seriously threatened by intensive agriculture, growing drinking water consumption in local towns and even overfishing. Thus, the fauna and flora are still endangered despite extensive preservation efforts. In the last fifty years alone, up to 90 percent of bird and 80 percent of fish species have died out.

Great blue herons, snakes, raccoons and frogs all feel at home in the marshy landscape of the Everglades (from left).

They say in Hawaii that when the lava flows, Pele, the goddess of fire, is angry. Nowhere else can you observe volcanic activity as intimately as on Hawaii's "Big Island", where two of the most active volcanoes in the world are part of the Hawaii Volcanoes National Park (main picture). Lava still pushes its way up from the depth of the oceans to the earth's surface.

The Polynesians, who came to Hawaii as early as 500 BC, called the islands "Heaven" or "Paradise". They would still be right. It is indeed a Garden of Eden for locals as well as visitors seeking a bit of tropical sunshine. The islands include Oahu, Kauai, Molokai, Lanai, Kahoolawe, Maui, and the Hawaii. At the time of the kings, who ruled the islands before they were usurped by the United States, traditional "chants" that told of life in the villages were still sung. Today, the hula, a dance in honor of the gods that was originally exclusively for men is still performed at various celebrations. Insets, from left: Excursion boats on the most famous beach in Hawaii, Waikiki in Honolulu on the island of Oahu; a tropical forest on Kauai; a surfer at Pipeline.

The Cathedral Metropolitana in Mexico City (main picture, top) is the largest religious building in the Americas. It dominates the Zócalo, the second-largest urban open space in the world. El Ángel (main picture, bottom), the golden angel at the Monumento a la Independencia, looks down over the Paseo de la Reforma from its 40-m (125-ft) column.

THE CAMPUS OF THE UNIVERSIDAD NACIONAL AUTÓNOMA DE MÉXICO

The first university in Latin America was founded in Mexico City in 1551 by King Philip II. Prior to being awarded autonomous status in 1929, the university originally comprised a collection of separate buildings in the historic heart of the city. It was only during the 1930s that plans were drawn up to building a university campus combining all of the institutes in one complex. The final plans were implemented from 1949 to 1952 at the Pedregal de San Ángel, then located outside the city. The master plan for the university's design was the work of architects Mario Pani and Enrique del Moral. Although they consistently applied the principles of contemporary architecture and modern urban development, they also managed to incorporate local traditions and building materials. Particularly remarkable is the successful integration within the architecture of works by artists such as Diego Rivera, José David Alfaro Siqueiros and others.

HISTORIC CENTER, XOCHIMILCO

According to unofficial figures, Mexico's capital is one of the fastest growing metropolitan areas in the world today. The metropolis lies at an altitude of 2,240 m (7,349 ft) above sea level, in a wide basin in the central highlands

From top to bottom: The National Palace, built in 1523 on the east side of the Zócalo; a giant mural by Diego Rivera inside the palace; the Palace of Fine Arts (above), built in the historic heart of Mexico City between 1904 and 1934, representative of the country's European heritage.

and on the site of the pre-Columbian city of Tenochtitlán. The former Aztec capital was founded in about 1370 on a number of islands in the Lago de Texcoco. Following the conquest of Tenochtitlán the city was almost completely destroyed by Spanish conquistadors in 1521. They then built their churches and colonial buildings on the ruins of where Aztec temples, palaces and sanc-

The university buildings embody tradition and modernity as well as the visual arts. The library by Juan O'Gorman (far left) and the rectorate tower by Enrique del Moral, Mario Pani and Salvador Ortega Flores (middle and left with a mural by Siqueiros) are typical examples.

tuaries once stood. Some of these heavy buildings, standing on typically soft, unstable ground, are now slowly threatened by subsidence. Aztec artefacts continue to be unearthed during construction work in the historical heart of Mexico.

A number of Mexico City's most significant historic buildings are grouped around the main square of Zócalo. The Templo Mayor, dedicated to the Aztec gods Tlaloc and Huitzilopochtli, is the most important relic from that era. The National Palace has been the scene of key political events and now serves as the president's residence. Paintings by Diego Rivera (1886–1957) depicting scenes from Mexico's history can be seen on the staircase and in an

Traces of the Aztec culture are still found today in the Templo Mayor (top) and in the "floating gardens" made of reed islands in Xochimilco (above).

upstairs gallery. The Metropolitana is the largest cathedral in the Americas and embodies a mix of styles from Renaissance to neoclassical. Magnificent patrician houses such as the Palacio de Marqués de Jaral de Berrio document Mexico's economic advancement. Architectural highlights of the 20th century include the Art Nouveau Palace of Fine Arts and the opera house, opened in 1937. The "floating gardens" (Chinampas) in Xochimilco, south of Mexico City, are today still reminiscent of the man-made water landscape created by the Aztecs in their capital Tenochtitlán.

The ruins of one of the most impressive Mayan cities are in the middle of the tropical jungle of Chiapas in southern Mexico. Although they had been discovered in 1784, the ruins of Palenque (main picture) were only systematically excavated in the 20th century.

CAMPECHE

Following it was founded in 1540, Campeche served as the starting point for the Spanish crown's conquest of the Yucatán. The important port soon became a lucrative target for notorious pirates such as Henry Morgan and William Parker, who plundered Campeche repeatedly. The hexagonal, over 2.5-km (1.8-mi) city wall was built between 1668 and 1704 and the defensive fortification with its four bastions ("baluartes") is one of the best-preserved in the Americas. Today the bastions and two forts house museums, galleries and botanical gardens. Exports of the red fabric dye, palo de tinte, is what inspired Campeche's second golden age in the 19th century and many magnificent buildings from this era have also survived: beautiful city palaces, the Teatro Toro, a number of churches built between 1540 and 1705, and the baroque but rather somber Catedrál de la Concepción San Francisquito, built on the site where the first mass is said to have been held in the New World in 1517.

PALENQUE

Palenque, a Mayan city that reached the zenith of its influence between the sixth and eighth centuries, was built between the third and the fifth centuries, when most important structures were erected. The glyphs in the Temple of the Inscriptions have been deciphered and constitute the most significant written records of Mayan culture. The untouched burial chamber of the Mayan Prince Pacal was discovered in the pyramid in 1952.

Directly adjacent to the "palace", with its high tower, is the Temple of the Inscriptions, a stepped pyramid with a temple construction on the roof platform (top). Almost all of the buildings are decorated with elaborate reliefs (bottom).

Inside the most famous temple, the 20-m-high (66-ft) Templo de las Inscripciones (Temple of the Inscriptions), are sixty steps leading into the crypt at a depth of 25 m (80 ft). Similar to the Egyptians, the Palenque pyramids were also burial chambers, the valuable objects from which are now on display in the Museo Nacional de Antropologíca in Mexico City. Opposite the Temple of the Inscriptions stands the "palace" where the royal family lived. Its 15-m (49-ft) tower was used for astronomy while a tabletop on the upper floor functioned as an altar.

The cathedral of Campeche (far left) is the oldest on the Yucatán Peninsula. The cobbled alleyways of the Old Town with its brightly colored buildings hold particular appeal (middle, left).

On March 21 and September 21, the sun falls on the giant El Castillo pyramid in Chichén Itzá in such a way that a shadow in the form of a serpent winds down the steps to meet a stone carved as a serpent's head at the bottom (main pictures, top). Below: A stone sentinel.

UXMAL

Uxmal, like the town adjacent to it, was an important urban and ceremonial center from the eighth to the 10th centuries. The central building is the almost 40 m (131 ft) high Pyramid of the Magician. The imposing construction, which was dedicated to the rain god Chac, is in fact the fourth building to have been constructed on this site of former temples. The expansive Governor's Palace stands on a 15-m-high (49-ft) platform decorated with an impressive stone mosaic frieze. The front elevations of the Nunnery, the House of the Tortoises and the Dovecote also feature detailed stone mosaics. The peculiar features of the friezes on the façade of the great palace of Sayil are surpassed only by those of the pillar ornaments. The triumphal arches over the once cobbled streets in Labná and Kabah are rare Mayan architectural treasures. The Palace of the Masks in Kabah owes its name to the roughly 250 stone masks of the god Chac on the front elevation. There is also a ball court in the complex.

CHICHÉN ITZÁ

These ruins extend over an area of 300 ha (741 acres) in the northern Yucatán and are the legacy of two pre-Columbian civilizations: the Maya and the Toltec. The cult site is thought to have been founded by the Maya in roughly 450. Large constructions followed in characteristically grand Mayan style such as the Complex of the Nuns or the main church. Groups influenced by the Toltec eventually moved into the abandoned Maya cult center in the 10th century and initiated a second golden age that lasted around 200 years. The transition to a Toltec-influenced

Chichén Itzá is characterized by a stylistic mix of ancient regional cultures with those of the Maya. The reclining figure here, known as "Chac Mool", in the Temple of the Warriors is an example (top). The skulls of those sacrificed were displayed (bottom) on a tzompantli, a foundation wall decorated with skull reliefs.

sculptural and relief style that featured warrior figures and graphic atlases is clearly recognizable. The observatory (Caracol) and the Quetzalcoatl pyramid known as the Castillo are representative of this epoch and have other monumental structures (Temple of the Jaguar) as well as a variety of ball courts grouped around them.

Situated on a giant platform, the Governor's Palace (main picture, in the foreground) is a masterpiece of Mayan architecture. Behind it stands the Pyramid of the Magician. Uxmal declined in importance from the 11th century and was finally abandoned by around 1200.

The longest-living barrier reef in the northern hemisphere is located off the coast of Belize on the edge of the continental shelf. It is made up of a variety of reef types comprising around sixty-five different coral species, their bizarrely shaped thickets and columns creating an ideal habitat for countless creatures. In addition to almost 250 species of aquatic plant this fantastic diversity also includes around 350 mollusk species, sponges, shellfish and about 500 fish species (above), from eagle rays to goliath groupers. Heavily endangered marine creatures such as manatees, hawksbill turtles and loggerhead sea turtles also inhabit this protected area. The islands (cayes) off the coast are mostly covered with either mangroves or palms. Accessible cayes in the area include Ambergris Caye, 58 km (36 mi) north of Belize City, and the Turneffe Islands. In addition to the underwater world, which often affords visibility of up to 30 m (65 ft), the reef's other attractions include the bird sanctuary on Half Moon Caye and the Blue Hole, a collapsed underwater cave.

Spectacular diving territory: the Blue
Hole (main picture), in the Belize Barrier
Reef 80 km (50 mi) east of Belize City.
These coral reefs were described by
Charles Darwin as early as 1842. An
underwater cave collapsed here around
10,000 years ago when the land sank
into the ocean. The circular "blue hole"
with a diameter of 300 m (328 yds) is
125 m (410 ft) deep.

The Agua Volcano rises steeply behind the Arco de Santa Catalina in Antigua Guatemala. Despite earthquake damage, the former capital of Guatemala is one of the loveliest Spanish colonial-style cities in the world (main picture).

ANTIGUA GUATEMALA

TIKAL

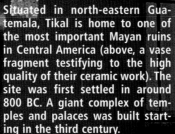

The Spanish conquerors founded the "noble" and "royal" city of Antigua in the highlands of Guatemala at the foot of three volcanoes in 1543 – the former settlement here had been destroyed in a mudslide. During the decades that followed, the capital of the Spanish colonial empire in Mesoamerica, situated at an altitude of 1,500 m (4,922 ft), developed into a virtual metropolis with up to 70,000 inhabitants. San Carlos de Borromeo, the first papal university in Central America, was founded here in 1675.

Built in Italian Renaissance style, Antigua, with its checkerboard layout, flourished for two centuries before being destroyed by an earthquake in 1773. The impressive ruins and rebuilt churches, cathedrals, monasteries, palaces and townhouses are testimony to the city's former economic, cultural and clerical significance. Today, the grandiose baroque colonial buildings still make it possible to see why Antigua (above: an Easter procession) was considered the loveliest capital in the New World.

Situated in north-eastern Guatemala, Tikal is home to one of the most important Mayan ruins in Central America (above, a vase fragment testifying to the high quality of their ceramic work). The site was first settled in around 800 BC. A giant complex of temples and palaces was built starting in the third century.

Tikal is located in a national park that covers around 600 sq km (232 sq mi) in the middle of a primeval forest that is home to a great many animals. During Tikal's golden age (550–900), up to 90,000 people lived in this temple city. To date, more than 3,000 buildings and complexes have been excavated in the 15-sq-km (6-sq-mi) area that was the city center – magnificent palaces as well as simple huts and ball courts. The most spectacular are the five gigantic temple pyramids, one of which is 65 m (213 ft) high and is the highest of all Maya constructions. In about the year 800 this cult site comprised twelve temples all built on one giant platform. Archeologists have also unearthed implements, cult items and burial objects.

QUIRIGUÁ

Monumental columns and elaborate calendars are among the
highlights of the archeological
site of Quiriguá in the remote
eastern corner of Guatemala,
close to the border with Honduras.
The first inhabitants settled here
in about AD 200, but this Mayan
city did not reach the height of
its prosperity until the eighth and
ninth centuries, a fact that is
reflected in a wealth of art treasures from the time. Like many
Mayan cities, however, Quiriguá
was then abandoned for centuries
for reasons unknown.

One important turning point in
the history of this city came during
the regency of Cauac Sky (right,
depicted on a column) with the
beheading of the mighty ruler
of Copán in 738, upon whom
Quiriguá had been politically
dependent for many years.

The city, its prosperity being
mostly based on the trade in
goods such as jade and obsidian,
consequently rose to become a
center of political power. The
majority of the famous monumental stelae date from this golden
age in the eighth century. The
elaborate and finely worked
sculptures on the monolithic
sandstone blocks are sculptural
masterpieces and depict political
and military events – including
the very execution on the main
square mentioned above that led
to the city's rise.

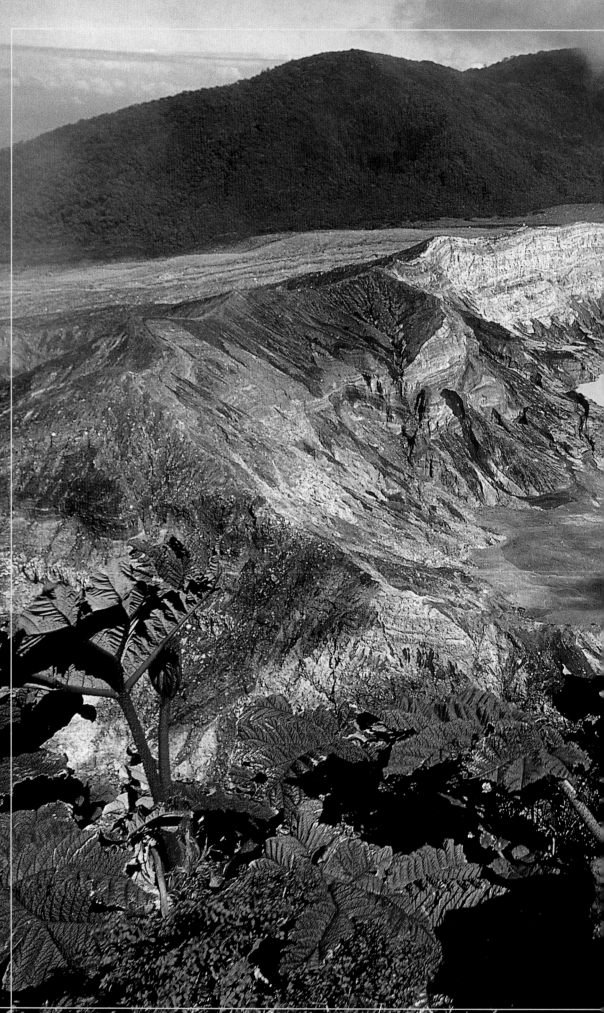

Poas Volcano is 2,704 m (8,872 ft) high and has two crater lakes. The water in the one is cold and clear while the lower crater (main picture) is an acidic lake with a diameter of 1,300 m (4,000 ft) and a depth of 300 m (963 ft). Sulfuric gas is emitted continually while the water shoots up like a geyser.

Geographically, Central America begins at the Mexican Isthmus of Tehuantepec, but there is a major geological border further to the east: the North American and Caribbean plates meet almost directly on the border between Guatemala and Honduras/El Salvador. This means that the land bridge from Honduras to South America is "Caribbean", which is indeed true of its climate (with few exceptions) and makes its plant and animal biodiversity unequalled anywhere in the world. Species from North and South America that once developed independently of one another intermingle here, for example. Cultural exchanges between the Mexican civilizations and South America also took place via the continental bridge which, at the Panama Canal, is only 46 km (29 mi) wide.

The volcanoes of the Cordillera Central and the Cordillera de Talamanca rise to an elevation of more than 3,400 m (11,155 ft) to the south of a gigantic rift, filled in part by the expansive Lago de Nicaragua. Some of them are still active like the 1,633-m (5, 358-ft) Arenal Volcano (main picture) in Costa Rica. This is due to the pressure exerted by the Pacific Cocos Continental Plate, which is sliding below the Caribbean Plate on the southern Costa Rican coast.

Tiny Costa Rica has a number of national parks within a relatively small area that are all still climatically very different: from the humid, tropical Caribbean side to the arid regions in the Pacific side, and from the marsh areas in the east to the rain forests of the central highlands and the dry forests of the north-west with its prickly bushes. Both coasts of the country also serve as breeding grounds for sea turtles, the inspiration for the Tortuguero National Park, which is only accessible by boat.

The Arenal Volcano (left), situated at the southern end of the lake of the same name and surrounded by a belt of tropical rainforest, is one of seven active volcanoes that rise out of the Cordillera Central, which traverses the country from the north-west to the southeast. Costa Rica's spectacular mountains of fire are situated east of the island's capital San José, on the edge of the Valle Central. Some of them have crater lakes such as Irazú and Poás, which feature geyser-like eruptions of muddy water and steam. Arenal erupted again in 1968 after being dormant for centuries and the crater now emits a constant plume of smoke.

GUANACASTE

This region in north-western Costa Rica covers 100,000 ha (247,100 acres) and comprises three national parks and smaller protected areas. It extends from the Pacific coast over the 2,000-m (6,562-ft) mountains of the interior down to the lowlands on the Caribbean side. Guanacaste encompasses coastal waters, islands, sandy beaches and coastal cliffs as well as streams and rivers in mountainous and volcanic landscapes, including the active composite volcano Rincón de la Vieja. No less than thirty-seven areas of wetland, mangroves and tropical rainforest are found here as well as tropical dry forest (in the background above) where the trees shed leaves during the hot season. This last remaining area of intact tropical dry forest in Central America measures around 60,000 ha (148,260 acres) and is one of the largest protected forest areas of its kind in the world.-

COCOS ISLAND

Cocos Island (in Spanish, *Isla del Coco*) is 550 km (342 mi) off the south-west coast of Costa Rica and boasts magnificent natural resources and tropical rain forests. Its isolated location has meant that numerous endemic plant species have been able to thrive here. There are also three bird, two reptile and more than sixty endemic insect species. The island's coastal waters are also part of a national park and are home to large fringing reefs with thirty-two coral species as well as a wealth of marine fauna. In addition to sharks (above, a scalloped hammerhead shark) there are another 300 fish species living in these waters.

The Talamanca and La Amistad reserves provide the ideal habitat for around 250 reptiles and amphibians as well as more than 200 mammals including the jaguar (main picture), puma, ocelot and tapir.

TALAMANCA AND LA AMISTAD

The cross-border reserve shared by Costa Rica and Panama boasts the greatest biodiversity of fauna and flora in the world. It covers the Central Cordillera de Talamanca from southern Costa Rica to western Panama and ranges from sea level all the way up to an elevation of roughly 3,800 m (12,468 ft). The wide spectrum of very diverse habitats and landscapes is predominantly covered with tropical rain forest, which has been growing here for 25,000 years (below). Above the lowlands are cloud forests and areas of sub-alpine paramo with bushes and grasses as well as areas with evergreen oaks, moors and lakes. Its topographic and climatic variety as well as its geographic location at the juncture between North and South America mean that the park has no shortage of unique flora and fauna. In addition to diverse finches, hawks and eagles, the vibrant acorn woodpeckers that benefit from the park's oak trees (above middle) contribute to the diversity of the indigenous bird species. The lovely long-tailed silky flycatchers (above right) live in montane forests above 1,800 m (5,906 ft). The magnificent quetzals (above left) are also among the region's feathered inhabitants. Archeological finds even indicate that human beings had been living in this region thousands of years ago but the research is still in its early stages. Today around 10,000 members of the indigenous Teribe, Guaymí, Bribri and Cabécar ethnic groups live in reserves located within the protected area.

HAVANA

"Queen of the Caribbean" is just one of Havana's epithets (above, the Malecón). Pastel hues envelop the city and the romanticism of "son" rhythms fill the air while flaking plaster walls play the bolero of decay. At Havana's legendary Tropicana nightclub (right), Cuba's most beautiful women dance in the most exotic of costumes. Indeed, Havana is not only one of the oldest but also one of the most fascinating cities in the New World. To protect the merchant harbor, where all the gold and silver transports were shipped from the Americas back to Spain, the Spanish built mighty fortifications between the 16th and the 18th centuries. The Old Town was

laid out in a checkerboard plan in which the grid of streets is frequently broken up by spacious squares. The main square, Plaza de Armas, features impressively restored colonial buildings such as the Palacio del Segundo Cabo. One of the most attractive baroque structures is the Palacio

de los Capitanes Generales. Also worth seeing are the old palaces of the former nobility with their wrought-iron balconies. Among the religious buildings in town, the Cathedral (above right) stands out. Completed in 1704, Alejo Carpentier once called it "music that has become stone". Right: A staircase in the Old Town.

VIÑALES

Bizarrely shaped *mogotes*, steep cone-shaped rocks created 150 million years ago, rise out of the valley in Viñales. They were once part of an extensive cave system that has since collapsed – what remains are the rock formations that lie in the valley like gigantic boulders. It is the main tobacco-growing region of Cuba.

Main picture: Havana is teeming with
classic cars, many of them lovingly done
up and used as taxis in Cuba.

CANAIMA

In the language of the Camarocoto Indians who live here, the name "Canaima" represents a somewhat sinister god who manifests all evil within himself. By contrast, the national park – which covers about 3 million ha (7.4 million acres), the second-largest in Venezuela – captivates with its overwhelming positive natural beauty. Located in the south-east of the country, on the borders with Guyana and Brazil, the park extends across the magnificent landscape of the Gran Sabana. It is fille with dense vegetation and spectacular waterfalls such as the Salto Ángel, the Salto Kukenam and the cascades of the Canaima Lagoon, which plunge over breathtaking cliffs. Between 3,000 and 5,000 species of flowering plants and ferns are said to exist here – many of them indigenous. Aside from savannah it also features impenetrable montane forests and scrubland. On the many *tepuy*, or flat-topped mountains, a special, even enterprising

vegetation has developed that includes carnivorous plants. Of the roughly 900 plant species that have been recorded on one of these *tepuys*, at least one-tenth are indigenous. Colorful butterflies, hummingbirds and parrots flutter through these forests while on the ground, mammals like great anteaters, giant arma-

dillos, giant otters, forest dogs and ocelots prowl around. The Catalan Captain Félix Cardona Puig was the first white man to see the powerful Salto Ángel waterfall in 1927. It was ultimately named after the American pilot, Jimmy Angel, however, who flew there in 1933, with his single-engine propeller plane.

The highest waterfall in the world, Salto Ángel (main picture and inset), plunges some 1,000 m (3,281 ft) from the north-eastern side of the roughly 2,500-m-high (8,202-ft) Auyántepui.

About 1,000 km (625 mi) off the west coast of Ecuador, out in the middle of the Pacific Ocean, is a spot where hot magma from the core of the earth developed into a spectacular archipelago consisting of twelve larger and more than 100 smaller volcanic islands. The oldest in the eastern-most part developed some 2.4 to 3 million years ago. Fernandina, in the west of the archipelago, is the youngest island, notching up just 700,000 years. Three major ocean currents flow around the archipelago including the Humboldt Current, which brings cold water from the icy polar regions right up to the Equator. Other currents bring life from the tropical and subtropical regions of Central and South America as well as the Indo-Pacific region, all of which have made the Galapagos Islands a swirling melting pot of the most diverse species. The geographic isolation of the archipelago also offered the optimum conditions for flora and fauna to develop in complete isolation. Charles Darwin's visit in 1835 ensured the enduring worldwide fame of the islands. Observing species of finches here that were nearly identical but which had developed different beak shapes according to the specific island they were on allowed him to gain valuable insights for the development of his theory of evolution. The Galapagos archipelago is a paradise for birds and reptiles alike, but very few mammals have managed to make their way there. In fact, most of the animals living on this group of islands are indigenous. Particularly spectacular species include the flightless cormorant, the Galapagos land iguana, the marine iguana, and of course the graceful and beautiful Galapagos tortoise.

Primeval species such as the Galápagos land iguana (main picture) were able to thrive on the remote Galapagos Islands off the coast of Ecuador. Galapagos tortoises (left), the largest living tortoises, can reach a weight of more than 200 kg (441 lbs). Marine iguanas (far left) feed on anything they find in the sea.

The first white person to discover Machu Picchu was the American Hiram Bingham in 1835. Bingham called the settlement Machu Picchu, meaning "Old peak", in reference to its location below the Huayna Picchu, or "Young peak". Simply put, everything seems mysterious about this Inca settlement, which sits like an eagle's eyrie on top of a flat mountain at an altitude of 2,430 m (7,973 ft) and is hidden in the tropical montane forest of the eastern Andes. What makes this place above the Río Urubamba Valley so fascinating is not just the amazingly well-pre-served buildings but also the unique harmony between architecture and nature. The structures are perfectly adapted to the uneven terrain around them. Speculation continues to this day as to the significance of this town, which was never discovered or even noticed by the Spanish colonists. Perhaps it was no more than an attempt by the Inca to also colonize the easterly slopes of the Andes. All that is certain is that the city was built around 1450 and abandoned again just one hundred years later. The complex is divided into two areas: the agricultural zone out on the steep mountain slopes, with terraces for arable farming that were integrated into a sophisticated irrigation system, and the unfortified urban district with palaces, temples and residential buildings. Among the most remarkable structures are the Round Tower, the Sun Temple and the Temple of the Three Windows.

Main picture: One of the best examples of perfectly integrating architecture with its surroundings is the "Forgotten City" of Machu Picchu, situated in a high-altitude landscape of stunning beauty. The Inca settlement, also known as the "City of the clouds", was built on several terraces on a high plateau.

CUZCO

The giant stone blocks of the Inca fortress of Sacsayhuamán (main picture), above Cuzco, look as if they were stacked by the hands of giants. It is still not certain how the blocks, some weighing more than 200 metric tons, were brought here – the Incas had no wheels or rollers.

Cuzco is one of the oldest cities in the New World that still exists today. This region was already settled by farming peoples in about 1000 BC, and about 2,000 years later it became the focal point of the powerful Inca Empire. According to one creation myth, the city, located at 3,400 m (11,155 ft) above sea level, is said to have been founded in about 1200 by Manco Cápac, the first mythical Inca ruler of the Kingdom of Cuzco. Over the 300 years or so that followed, Cuzco developed into the most sumptuous Inca city in the empire and became the political, religious and cultural heart of their realm. Most of the temples and palaces were built during this imperial period, which began with the accession to power of King Pachacútec (1438). It is said that numerous buildings were clad in gold and copper plates. In 1533, the conquistador Francisco Pizarro brutally conquered the city. Cuzco was destroyed and missionaries built their churches and monasteries on top of the ruins of the Inca temples in order to extirpate the memories of indigenous traditions.

A view cross the rooftops towards the Cathedral of Cuzco (left), built in the 17th century in the Renaissance style.

Main picture: Jaú National Park, Mamirauá and Amanã nature reserves, and Anavilhanas Ecological Station encompass the largest protected area of rainforest in the Amazon Basin. The region's dense tropical rain forest and floodplain forests are one of the most biodiverse areas on earth.

MANAUS

The capital of the Brazilian state of Amazonas is situated on the banks of the Rio Negro, in the heart of the rain forest. Founded in 1669 as a Portuguese fort, Manaus developed into a flourishing metropolis during the rubber boom at the turn of the 20th century but increased use of synthetic rubber products then caused a dramatic downturn in the city's prosperity. It was only after Manaus was declared a free trade zone in 1967 that it once again recovered from the decades of decline. The city is the seat of the Universidade Federal do Amazonas, established in 1965, and plays an important role in regional tourism as the jumping off point for excursions into the Amazon basin. Reminders of the rubber boom include the market halls (Mercado Municipal Adolfo Lisboa), which were built in a cluster around the port in 1902, their cast-iron construction a Gustave Eiffel design; and the Palácio Rio Negro (1910), a well-preserved city villa that once housed the regional government and today serves as a cultural center for visitors. The famous opera house, the Teatro Amazonas, towers gracefully over the port (above), its dome decorated with 36,000 ceramic tiles that were imported from Alsace, France. Although the theater was officially opened on December 31, 1896, it wasn't actually completed until 1898.

The Amazon is by far the largest river system on earth: its catchment area alone is larger than Western Europe. The river is only called the Amazon after its confluence with the Rio Negro 18 km (11 mi) downstream from Manaus. In its middle reaches it is called the Solimõe, into which three tributaries flow: the Maranón, the Huallaga and the Ucayali, all of which rise in the Andes. The other tributaries – the Rio Negro, Río Madeira, Rio Tapajós and Rio Xingu – are of great size as well. The difference between the ebb and flow in the Amazon can be up to 15 m (49 ft). After Manaus the river is very sluggish and seldom less than 5 km (3 mi) wide, except near Óbidos where it narrows to 2 km (1.2 mi) and can reach depths of 100 m (328 ft). Scientists have theorized that the source of the primeval Amazon was originally in what is today the Sahara. What has been proven is the fact that the river originally flowed in the opposite direction, namely into the Pacific. South America and Africa, then one continent, began to split apart 70 million years ago. The upthrust of the Andes then began at the same time as the American Plate slid westward under the East Pacific Plate. For a long time the river flowed westward through Guayaquil. The current direction only dates from about six million years ago. In general, the soils of the Amazon rain forest region – the largest continuous forest area on earth – are oddly low in nutrients, making human encroachment an issue. Intentional fires to clear land as well as unregulated logging have forced the government to put huge areas under protection – often unsuccessfully. When Europeans arrived in about 1500, there were about two million Indians here; today they number no more than 50,000. Whole tribes were decimated, enslaved, or succumbed to epidemics introduced by colonists.

Insets, clockwise from top left: Dense Amazon rainforest; an ocelot, under threat from fur hunters; Kayapó Indians; the Rio Negro at a width of 2 km (1.2 mi) near Manaus; Yanomami Indians. The Brazilian Federal Indian Bureau FUNAI is committed to protecting indigenous Amazon peoples.

Main picture: "God created the world in six days; the seventh day he dedicated to creating Rio" – the pride of Rio's inhabitants is perhaps most gloriously and colorfully expressed during Carnival.

When Portuguese seafarer André Gonçalvez arrived with his ships in expansive Guanabara Bay on January 1, 1502, he thought he had discovered an estuary. As a result, he called what he thought to be a river the Rio de Janeiro – January River. Very few cities in the world enjoy a location and a backdrop as breathtaking as Rio de Janeiro. Together with the 394-m (1,293-ft) Sugar Loaf mountain (above right), the famous statue of Christ with outstretched arms on top of the 704-m (2,310-ft) Corcovado mountain (above) is one of the most recognizable icons in the metropolis – if not in the world.

Founded on March 1, 1564, as the Cidade de São Sebastião do Rio de Janeiro, Rio is not only Brazil's former capital, but also the former capital of the Portuguese Empire. Right on the Atlantic, Rio boasts two of the world's most famous beaches: Copacabana and Ipanema (below).

IGUAÇU

The locals call the Iguaçu Falls "Garganta del Diablo" (the Devil's Throat). The massive falls cascade over a number of wide precipices in an area where dense vegetation covers even the smallest of islands in the Iguaçu River (main picture).

Iguaçu Falls, where Brazil, Argentina and Paraguay meet, can be heard long before they actually come into view. Initially it is a faint gurgling that quickly swells into a deafening, thunderous roar. The Iguaçu River, lined with dense tropical vegetation and called the Iguazú in Argentina, is about 1 km (0.6 mi) wide where it approaches the horseshoe-shaped precipice. The falls then crash with impressive power over a cliff that is 2,700 m (850 ft) in length – an amazing natural spectacle. More than 270 individual waterfalls have been counted here.

The adjacent Iguaçu National Park on the Brazilian side covers an area of 1,700 sq km (656 sq mi) and provides refuge for a vast range of endangered species. Parrots and white-bellied nothuras flit around under the protection of dense forests while swifts build their nests in the craggy rocks between the waterfalls. This rain forest region is also home to jaguars, tapirs, ant bears and collared peccaries. Both the Argentinian and Brazilian sides were made UNESCO World Heritage Sites in the 1980s.

Iguaçu means "big water" in the language of the indigenous Guaraní Indians. Sunlight shines through the spray creating an enchanting rainbow (left) as almost two tons of water per second plunge into the gorge with a deafening roar.

LAKE TITICACA

Lake Titcaca can make some unique claims: with a surface area of 8,300 sq km (204 sq mi), it is the largest lake in South America; it straddles the border between Peru and Bolivia; and it lies at an elevation of 3,812 m (12,507 ft), the highest commercially navigable lake in the world. In addition to that, the natural landscape and the Inca ruins in the region around the lake are a

source of ceaseless fascination. The Isla del Sol, for example, contains Inca cultural and ritual sites. According to Inca legend, the island is the birthplace of the sun god. The Temple of the Sun (Templo del Sol), situated on the highest point of the island, is particularly shrouded in mystery. The Island of the Moon (Isla de la Luna) is also worth a visit. Beyond the geological islands on Lake Tit-

icaca, there are also a number of man-made floating islands on the lake (left). They were created in pre-Inca times by the Uros (Uru), fisher folk who live on these artificial islands. Initially they used reeds mixed with earth just to build the foundations of their houses on land. The continual rise in the water level, however, meant that they had to keep raising these foundations until some

of the houses began floating on the lake during the floods. Since this had advantages for fishing, the Uros decided to make a virtue out of necessity – the concept also afforded them protection from Inca attacks. The Uros simply retreated to their floating islands on the lake whenever there was threat of an invasion. The Uros also use reeds to make their stylized boats (below).

Lake Titicaca (main picture) in the Peruvian-Bolivian highlands is located at an elevation of 3,812 m (12,507 ft), and is 190 km (118 miles) long and 50 km (31 mi) wide.

ALTIPLANO

Western Bolivia is a high-elevation region dominated by impressive mountain ranges with expansive basins stretching between them. This contrast is especially visible along the border with Chile. The basin landscape of the Altiplano (literally meaning "high level") extends between the Cordillera Occidental (Western Cordillera) and the Cordillera Oriental (Eastern Cordillera) of the Andes and where elevations range between 3,600 and 4,200 m (11,812 and 13,780 ft). The 6,520-m (20,506-ft) Mount Sajama (left, with a church built of air-dried bricks in the foreground) in the national park of the same name is an eye catcher that is visible from great distances. With a permanent snowcap above 5,300 m (17,389 ft), Mount Sajama is a dormant volcano, but there is a very high degree of tectonic activity in the region, and volcanic eruptions and earthquakes are a frequent occurrence.

CORDILLERA REAL

This region is indeed worthy of the lofty name. Cordillera Real (or Royal Cordillera) is a fascinating range that extends east from Lake Titicaca, in Bolivian territory (above), its glistening high-altitude glaciers visible from afar when the sun is shining. In addition to the highest peak in the range, the 6,880-m (22,573-ft) Nevado del Illimani (above), there are a number of other peaks here that break the 6,000 m (19,686 ft) mark. They are so spectacular that passionate mountaineers from all over the world travel to South America to trek in the Cordillera Real.

TORRES DEL PAINE, LAUCA, ALERCE ANDINO

The granite peaks of the Chilean Torres del Paine (main picture) tower 3,050 m (10,007 ft) over the Southern Patagonian plains.

TORRES DEL PAINE

The mountains of the Torres del Paine range rise directly from the expansive, windswept plain. They consist of steep, seemingly impregnable peaks and massive granite formations with the 3,050-m (10,007-ft) Cerro Torre Grande as their highest point. Cerro Torre is then surrounded by the only slightly lower peaks of Paine Chico, Torres del Paine and Cuernos del Paine. This national park is Chile's adventure paradise and offers a wide range of hiking trails for both short day tours or longer treks that take visitors through the entire park and last several days. All of these fascinating excursions bring you through the glorious glacial landscape, over the Grey Glacier and along the swift-moving Río Paine river, which cascades into Lago Pehoe lake. Gnarled trees bracing themselves against the wind are a unique feature of the park, as are the colorful plains covered in wildflowers, endangered Andean condors, various waterfowl and endemic guanacos. Any trip to this region requires good preparation.

LAUCA

Chile is "an island on the mainland". To the north it is bordered by the world's driest desert, in the west by the waves of the Pacific and in the east by the peaks of the Andes. To the south, Chile dissolves into an array of islands that are then lost in the Antarctic Ocean. Lauca National Park is home to a number of permanently snow-capped, 6,000-m (19,686-ft) peaks that include superb volcanoes such as Parinacota (above) at 6,342 m (20,808 ft) as well as Lago Chungará, one of the highest lakes on earth.

ALERCE ANDINO

Alerce Andino National Park extends along the Seno and the Estuario de Reloncaví and is home to ancient conifers (related to the redwoods) that reach diameters of up to 4 m (13 ft) and heights of up to 50 m (164 ft). Many of the trees are around 1,000 years old. The famous Carretera Austral, Chile's loveliest route into the solitude of the south, also begins near Puerto Montt in Alerce Andino. This mixed paved and gravel road stretches along more than 1,000 km (621 mi) of rural Patagonia through forest and past lakes, fjords and snow-covered peaks. Some 100,000 people live in this wild region.

The granite peaks of Torres del Paine National Park in Chile rise up from the plains of Southern Patagonia like an impregnable fortress (left).

The heart of the Atacama Desert is the driest place in the world. The Humboldt Current, an ocean current off the Pacific coast, carries cold water from the Antarctic northward. Due to the lack of wind, the steep coastal mountains then trap fog rising from the ocean – and therefore the moisture – which keeps it from reaching the interior. This results in an extremely dry climate, with some places having never recorded any form of precipitation since records have been taken. To put it mildly, it is an inhospitable environment that can be very warm during the day and uncomfortably cold at night. Yet it is anything but monotonous. The ocher desert mountains and snow-covered volcanoes are as enchanting as the deep blue and green lagoons and the scattered oases. Above right is a salt lake in the Atacama with stratovolcanoes in the background. In the center is one of the loveliest of these, Licancábur at 5,916 m (19,410 ft). To the right is the Géiser el Tatio geyser field, which is typically at its most active in the early morning.

A booming economy does not always require a fertile landscape. The desert, too, has its riches. In this case, these riches made Chile a wealthy country back in the 19th century, initially with saltpeter, an essential raw material for the manufacture of gunpowder and artificial fertilizers. At that time, however, the Atacama did not yet belong to Chile. This vast region was shared by Peru and Bolivia, Chile having become involved in the saltpeter business only through a company in Antofagasta. In 1879, when the Bolivian government made an attempt to expropriate the

company, Chile made its move. The army occupied the town, instigating the Saltpeter War. Peru and Bolivia lost the war in 1883 and Chile then enjoyed a saltpeter monopoly. Most of the towns are derelict nowadays, but

new towns continue to appear elsewhere in the desert: Chuquicamata, for instance, not far from Calama. This small town was built up around the world's largest opencast copper mine. The vast, man-made crater is

At 6,893 m (22,616 ft), the Ojos del Salado (main picture), located in the Atacama Desert on the border between Argentina and Chile, is one of the highest volcanoes on earth as well as one of the tallest peaks in the Andes.

4 km (2.5 mi) long, 2 km (1.2 mi) wide and about 700 m (2,297 ft) deep. Several hundred thousand tons of rock are blasted here every day before being loaded onto giant trucks, crushed and washed. The mine generates one million tons of pure copper (99.6 percent) annually along with smaller quantities of valuable minerals, including gold and silver. Chuquicamata is expected to yield copper until beyond 2010 before the deposits become exhausted. The Chileans are optimistic, however: Other copper mines will replace them and the desert also holds other mineral reserves including sulfur, phosphate, gold, silver, manganese, molybdenum, rhenium and lithium. San Pedro de Atacama is the best jumping off point for exploring this impressive desert region (below right, the Adobe church in San Pedro). About 12 km (7.5 mi) to the west is the Valle de la Luna (above left) a bizarre, waterless erosion landscape created primarily by wind (since there is no precipitation). "Moon valley" is most impressive at sunset and at full moon when the sandstone glows in all manner of colors, from ocher-yellow and orange to deep red and violet, with everything bathed in pale white moonlight. Almost 100 km (62 mi) north of San Pedro de Atacama is the Géiser el Tatio geyser field. These geysers are really a sight for early risers. To reach the geysers, which should be visited before sunrise because it is only at dusk and in the early morning hours that they are at their most active, visitors must take a poor dirt road that leads past Licancábur volcano (5,916 m/19,410 ft). Bubbling up from dozens of holes in this volcanic landscape, they make for a fascinating spectacle against the clear blue sky of the rising sun. The geysers are situated at an altitude of 4,300 m (14,108 ft), making it one of the highest geyser fields in the world. The salt lake south of San Pedro covers an area of 3,000 sq km (1,158 sq mi). It is no shiny, white salt lake, but rather a crusty, brown-white clay mixture interspersed with salt crystals. There are a number of individual water basins in the lake, however, that form small, clear lagoons that are often frequented by flamingos. These lagoons are also at their best at sunset when the Salar shimmers in a variety of pastel tones and the flamingos stand as dark silhouettes in the water. The best view can be enjoyed at Lago Chaxa, which is about 50 km (31 mi) south of San Pedro. Above are the salt pans of the Atacama Desert.

RAPA NUI (EASTER ISLAND)

The tuff statues, some of which are several meters high, are impressive testimony to a lost Polynesian civilization on Rapa Nui, an island in the middle of the Pacific that measures just 164 sq km (63 sq mi) and belongs to Chile (main picture).

Two million years ago the Rano Kau volcano rose up out of the vast Pacific Ocean. The island that this uplifting created originally comprised seventy-seven smaller craters. At a distance of some 3,700 km (2,299 mi) from the South American mainland and around 4,200 km (2,610 mi) from Tahiti, Easter Island) is one of the most isolated places on earth.

The island was first settled as early as AD 400. A second wave of settlement is thought to have taken place in the 14th century, when the legendary King Hotu Matua arrived here with his Polynesian followers. The Polynesians called the island Rapa Nui, meaning "Big island". The main testaments to their culture are the several hundred "moais", tuff sculptures, measuring up to 10 m (33 ft) in height and standing on large platforms known as "ahu", and the Rongorongo script, a kind of pictorial writing. The significance of the moais has not yet been established. Dutchman Jacob Roggeveen reached the island, which is today inhabited by about 4,000 people, on Easter Monday 1722, which gave the island its present name.

The function or meaning of the *moais* – gigantic figures and heads made of tuff that were erected on Easter Island (left and far left) – remains a mystery.

Main picture: The Plaza de la Republica
is one of the most popular nightspots in
Buenos Aires. The 67-m (220-ft) obelisk at
its center commemorate the founding of
the city in 1536.

Porteños – or port residents – is what the residents of Buenos Aires call themselves, referring to the city's location on the western side of the Río de la Plata. Around three million people live in the city of "good air" (above a mural in the port district of La Boca), and almost fourteen million in the greater urban area – about one-third of the entire Argentinean population, which is of largely European descent. Founded by the Spanish in 1536 as Nuestra Señora Santa María del Buen Aire, the city had to be abandoned just five years later following bloody conflicts with indigenous populations. It was founded anew in 1580, was the capital of a Spanish viceroyalty from 1776 to 1810, and has been the capital of Argentina since 1880. The heart of the metropolis, with its grid layout, is the Plaza de Mayo with the Casa Rosada, seat of the state president. The Mothers of the Plaza de Mayo gather there on Thursday afternoons in silent protest against the crimes committed by the military dictatorship. Buenos Aires became famous as the birthplace of the tango (above) – "a sad thought that is danced", according to the Argentinean composer Enrique Santos Discepolo in his description of the "dance of the emotions", characterized by sensual passion and eroticism.

LOS GLACIARES

Main picture: The front of the Perito Moreno Glacier rises up to 60 m (197 ft) above Lago Argentino. Ice blocks are continually breaking off and crashing into the sea.

The park's thirteen glaciers form part of the Patagonian Ice Field which, covering 15,000 sq km (5,790 sq mi), is the largest continuous ice mass outside of Antarctica. There are also another 200 small glaciers not directly connected to the ice field. The most famous of these is the 30-km-long (19-mi), 5-km-wide (3-mi) Perito Moreno Glacier, which slowly pushes its "tongue" across a peninsula, cutting off a branch of Lago Argentino every three or four years. When the wall of ice is no longer able to withstand the pressure, the backed-up mass of water breaks through part of the glacier front and makes its way to the sea.

Bizarrely formed icebergs owing their ornate shapes to the harsh elements are a common sight south of the Antarctic Circle. Penguins often rest on them (right, main picture).

"It lies there, wilder than any other part of our earth, unseen and untouched," wrote Norwegian Roald Amundsen, the first person to reach the South Pole, in his travel journal in 1911. The Antarctic is a gigantic land mass almost completely covered with snow and ice. Only one-sixtieth of its surface area (with the ice shelf almost 14 million sq km/5.5 million sq mi) is free of ice while the rest is covered by ice with an average thickness of 2,500 m (8,203 ft) – it reaches thicknesses of over 4,500 m (14,765 ft) in spots. This ice expanse is not a flat surface either, but one that is traversed by high mountain ridges. One of the longest ranges on earth is found here, the Transantarctic Mountains, which extends diagonally across the continent over more than 4,800 km (2,983 miles). Only the highest peaks such as the 4,897-m (16,067-ft) Mount Vinson poke up through the gigantic ice mass. The Antarctic has never been truly settled by humans. The more than eighty research stations are home to about 4,000 people in the summer and about 1,000 in the winter.

King penguins are the second-largest penguin species and primarily inhabit the Sub-Antarctic Islands (left). They breed for the first time when they are six years old, the egg initially being incubated by the male in the folds of its belly. The incubation period lasts for a total of fifty-five days.

Location index

Abu SImbel 196
Agra 126
-, Taj Mahal 126
Aix-en-Provence 42
Alaska 232
Aleppo 106
Alerce Andino 290
Altiplano 288
Amazon 282
Amazon Basin 282, 283
Amboseli 200
Americas, The 224–300
Amrum 56
Amsterdam 32
Angkor 154
Antarctica 300
Antigua Guatemala 266
Antofagasta 292
Antwerp 34
Aoraki/Mount Cook 176
Arenal 268
Argentina 296–299
Arles 92, 93
Asia 104–163
Atacama 292
-, El Tatio Geyser 292
-, Salar de Atacama 293
-, Valle de la Luna 293
Athens 94
-, Acropolis 94
-, Dimotikí Agorá 95
-, Pláka 95
-, Psirrí 95
Australia 164–173
Austria 64–67
Avebury 24
Avignon 44

Bali 162
Bamiyan Valley 323
Bangkok 156
-, Chinatown 156
-, Grand Palace 156, 157
-, Wat Arun 157
-, Wat Pho 157
-, Wat Phra Kaeo 156
Barcelona 46, 47
-, Barri Gòtic, Gothic Quarter 47
-, Casa Batlló 47
-, Casa Milà 47
-, Casa Vicens 47
-, Colonia Güell 47
-, La Seu 47
-, La Boqueria 46
-, Palau de la Música 46
-, Palau Güell 47
-, Parque Güell 47
-, Placa del Rei 46
-, Rambles 46
-, Sagrada Familia 46, 47
Bat 117
Batu Caves 159
Beara 30
Beijing 136, 137
-, Changan Boulevard 136
-, Emperor's Palace 136
-, Forbidden City 136, 137
-, Summer Palace of Empress Cixi 137
-, Temple of Heaven 137
-, Tiananmen Square 136
Belgium 33, 34
Belize 264, 265
Belize Barrier Reef 264, 265
Ben Nevis 28
Bergen 14
Berlin 54, 55

-, Charlottenburg Castle 55
-, Kaiser Wilhelm Memorial Church 55
-, Kurfürstendamm 54
Bern 60
Białowieża 80
Blue Hole 264
Blue Mountains 170
Bolivia 288, 289
Bora Bora 180, 181
Borneo, Malaysia 160
Botswana 208, 209
Brazil 282–287
Bruges 34
Bryce Canyon 242, 243
Budapest 86, 87
-, Chain Bridge 87
-, Fisherman's Bastion 86
-, Gellért Baths 86
-, Heroes' Square 87
-, Matthias Church 86
-, Opera 87
-, Parliament 86
-, St Stephen's Basilica 87
Buenos Aires 296, 297

Cairo 192, 193
-, Al-Azhar 192
-, Egyptian Museum 193
-, Old Cairo 192
-, Khan El-Khalili 192
-, Mohammed-Ali 193
Camargue 45
Cambodia 154, 155
Campeche 620
Canada 226–231
Canaima 274, 275
Cannes 40, 41
Cap de Formentor 50, 51
Cape Town 214, 215
Casbah Trail 188
Chicago 248, 249
-, Chicago Blues 249
-, Chicago Tribune Tower 249
-, Skyline 248, 249
-, The Loop 248
Chichén Itzá 262, 263
Chile 290–295
China 136–145
Chobe 208
Chuquicamata 292
Cocos Island 270
Colorado River 246, 247
Copenhagen 18
-, Amalienborg 19
-, Cristiansborg 19
-, Frederikskirke church 19
-, Nyhaun 18
Cordillera Real 289
Costa Rica 268–271
Costa Smeralda 218
Croatia 88, 89
Cuba 272, 273
Cuzco 280, 281
Czech Republic 84, 85

Damascus 106, 107
Danube Delta 92, 93
Delhi 124, 125
-, Qutb-Minar 124
-, Red Fort 124, 125
-, Tomb of Humayun 125
Delphi 96
Denali 232
Denmark 18, 19
Dettifoss 12
Dingle 30
Drottningholm 16

Dubai 116, 117
Dubrovnik 90, 91

Ecuador 276–281
Edinburgh 26, 27
Egmont 174
Egypt 192–197
El Djem 190
El Escorial 48
Epidauros 96
Etosha 210, 211
Everglades 254

Fez 184
-, Kairaouine Mosque 184
-, Madrassa es-Sharij 185
-, Nejjarine Square 185
-, Old Town 184, 185
-, Royal Palace 184
-, Tannery Quarter 184
-, Tomb of Moulay Idriss II. 185
Fiji Islands 180, 181
Finland 20, 21
Fish River Canyon 213
Florida Keys 253
Föhr 56
France 36–45
French Polynesia 180
Frombork 78
Fuji-san, Mount Fuji 148, 149

Galapagos Islands 276, 277
Garden Route 216
Gates of the Arctic 232
Gdansk 78
Geirangerfjord 14, 15
Germany 64–59
Ghent 34, 35
Glencoe 28
Goðafoss 12
Golden Horn 98
Grand Canyon 246, 247
Great Barrier Reef 168, 169
Great Britain 22–29
Great Wall of China 138, 139
Greece 94–97
Guatemala 266, 267
Guilin 388
Gunung Mulu 160

Halong 150
Havana 272, 273
Hawaii 256, 257
Helgoland 156
Helsinki 20, 21
HIgh Atlas 89
Highlands 28, 29
Highway 1 572
Ho Chi Minh City (Saigon) 152
Hungary 86, 87
Hunza Valley 122, 123

Ibiza 51
Iceland 12, 13
Iguaçu Falls 286, 287
India 124–129
Indonesia 162, 163
Iran 118, 119
Ireland 30, 31
Isfahan 118, 119
Israel 108, 109
Istanbul 98, 99

-, Blue Mosque (Sultan Ahmed) 98
-, Galata Bridge 98, 99
-, Golden Horn 98
-, Yeni Cami Mosque 98
Italy 68–77
Iveragh 30

Jaipur 128, 129
-, City Palace 128, 129
-, Jantar Mantar 129
-, Johari Bazaar 128
-, Palace of the Winds 128, 129
-, Tripolia Bazaar 128
Japan 146, 147
Jerusalem 108, 109
-, Church of the Holy Sepulchre 109
-, Dome of the Rock 109
-, Jewish Quarter 108
-, Wailing Wall (Western Wall) 108
Jordan 110, 11

Kailash, Mount 145
Kairouan 190, 191
Kalahari 208, 209
Kamchatka 134, 135
Karakoram 122, 123
Karnak 194
Kata Tjuta 166, 167
Katherine Gorge 167
Kathmandu 130, 131
-, Boudhanath Stupa 130, 131
-, Swayambunath Temple 131
Kenya 200, 201
Kilimanjaro 204, 205
Killarney 31
Kobuk Valley 232
Kokerboom Forest 212
Kowloon 142
Krafla 12, 13
Kraków 82, 83
-, Corpus Christi Church 83
-, Jewish Quarter 82
-, St Mary's Church 83
-, Market Square (Rynek) 82, 83
Kuala Lumpur 158, 159
-, Petronas Towers 158, 159

La Amistad 270, 271
Las Vegas 238, 239
Lauca 290
Lhasa 144, 145
Lisbon 52, 53
-, Alfama 52
-, Bairro Alto 52
-, Baixa 52
-, Hieronymite Convent 53
-, Torre de Belém 52, 53
Lombok 162, 163
London 22, 23
-, Big Ben 22, 23
-, Buckingham Palace 22
-, Financial District 23
-, St. Paul's Cathedral 23
-, Tower of London 22, 23
-, Tower Bridge 22, 23
Los Glaciares 298, 299
Lubéron 42
Luxor 194

Macau 143
Machu Picchu 278, 279
Madagascar 218, 219
Madrid 49
-, Monasterio de las Calzas Reales 49

-, Museo del Prado 49
-, Nuestra Señora de la Almudena 49
-, Palacio Real 49
-, Plaza Mayor 49
-, San Francisco el Grande 49
Mahé 220, 221
Makgadikgadi 208, 209
Malar, Lake 16, 17
Malaysia 158–161
Malbork 78
Mali 198, 199
Mallorca 50, 51
Manaus 282
Marrakesh 186, 187
-, Bab Agnaou 187
-, Bahia Palace 187
-, Casbah 187
-, Djemaa el-Fna 186, 187
-, Koutoubia Mosque 186
-, Madrassa Ben Yusuf 187
-, Royal Palace 187
-, Saad tombs 187
-, Souks 187
Marseille 44
Maasai Mara 201
Masurian Lake District 80, 81
Matterhorn 62, 63
Mauritius 222, 223
Mecca 112, 113
Medina 113
Mekong Delta 153
Menorca 51
Mexico 258–263
Mexico City 258, 259
-, National Palace 258
-, Opera House 259
-, Palace of Fine Arts 258
-, Templo Mayor 259
-, Tenochtitlán 258
-, Universidad Nacional Autónoma
    de Mexico 258, 259
-, Xochimilco 258
-, Zócalo 259
Miami 252, 253
Miami Beach 252
Mont-Saint-Michel 38, 39
Montreal 230, 231
Monument Valley 244, 245
Morocco 184–189
Moscow 100, 101
-, GUM 101
-, Kremlin 100
-, Red Square 101
-, St Basil's Cathedral 101
Mount Everest (Sagarmatha) 132, 133
Mount Kinabalu 160, 161
Mount Ngauruhoe 174, 175
Mungo National Park 170
Munich 58
-, Frauenkirche (church) 58
-, Hofbräuhaus 59
-, Marienplatz 58
-, Nymphenburg Castle 59
-, Residence 58
Mycenae 96
Mývatn 13

Namib-Naukluft National Park 212
Namibia 210–213
Nepal 130–133
Netherlands 32, 33
New York City 250, 251
-, Broadway 251
-, Bronx 250
-, Brooklyn 250
-, Brooklyn Bridge 251
-, Central Park 251
-, Chinatown 250

-, Chrysler Building 251
-, Downtown 250
-, East Village 250
-, Empire State Building 251
-, Fifth Avenue 251
-, Greenwich Village 250
-, Harlem 251
-, Little Italy 250
-, Manhattan 250, 251
-, Midtown 251
-, Queens 250
-, SoHo 250
-, Staten Island 250
-, Times Square 250, 251
-, TriBeCa 250
-, UN Building 251
-, Uptown 251
New Zealand 174–177
Ngorongoro 202
Niagara Falls 228, 229
Nice 40
Nitmiluk 167
Normandy 38
Norway 14–15

Oceania 178–183
Ojos del Salado 292
Okavango Delta 208, 209
Olympia 96

Pakistan 122, 123
Palenque 260, 261
Palermo 76, 77
Panama 271
Papua New Guinea 178, 179
Paris 36, 37
-, Notre-Dame 36, 37
-, Sainte-Chapelle 37
Persepolis 120, 121
Peru 278–281
Petra 110, 111
Plitvicer Lakes 88, 89
Poás 268, 269
Poland 78–83
Pompeii 74, 75
Portugal 52, 53
Prague 84, 85
-, Charles Bridge 85
-, Golden Lley 84
-, Lesser Quarter 85
-, St Veits Cathedral 84
Pura Besakih 162

Quiriguá 267

Rannoch Moor 28
Rapa Nui (Easter Island) 294, 295
Redwood 235
Réunion Island 222, 223
Rio de Janeiro 284, 285
-, Copacabana 285
-, Ipanema 285
Romania 92, 93
Rome 68, 69
-, Capitol Hill 68, 69
-, Colosseum 69
-, Forum Romanum 68
-, Pantheon 69
Russia 100–103, 134, 135

Saint Michael's Mount 38
Saimaa 20
San Francisco 234, 235
-, Alamo Square 234
-, Chinatown 234
-, Fisherman's Wharf 234
-, Golden Gate Bridge 234, 235
Sana'a 114, 115
Saudi Arabia 112, 113
Serengeti 202, 203
Seychelles 220, 221
Shanghai 140, 141
-, Bund 141
-, Huangpu 141
-, Nanjing Lu 141
-, Pudong 140, 141
-, Yu Garden 141
Shibam 114
Sicily 76, 77
Simpson Desert 166
Sognefjord 15
Son Marroig 50
Sossusvlei 212, 213
South Africa 214, 215
Spain 46–51
St Petersburg 102, 103
-, Hermitage, Theater 102
-, Palace Square 103
-, Winter Palace 102, 103
Stockholm 16, 17
Stonehenge 24
Sweden 16, 17
Switzerland 60–63
Sydney 170
Sylt 56, 57

Table Mountain 214
Tanzania 202–205
Tasmania 172, 173
-, Flinders Island 172
-, East Coast 172
-, Tasmanian Wilderness 172
Thailand 156, 157
Tibet 144, 145
Tikal 266
Titicaca, Lake 288, 289
Tokyo 146, 147
Tongariro 174
Toronto 228, 229
-, BCE Place 228
-, CN Tower 229
-, Holy Trinity Church 228
-, Ontario Place 228
-, Yorkville 228
Torres del Paine 290, 291
Torun 78
Tunis 190
Tunisia 190, 191
Turkey 272–281

Uluru 166, 167
United Arab Emirates 116, 117
United Kingdom 22–29
United States of America 232–257

Vancouver 226, 227
Vancouver Island 226
Vatican 70, 71
-, Sistine Chapel 71
-, St Peter's Basilica 170, 171
Venezuela 274, 275
Venice 72, 73
-, Grand Canal 73
-, Palazzo Ducale 72
-, Rialto Bridge 73

-, San Giorgio Maggiore 72, 73
-, San Marco 72
Victoria Falls 206, 207
Vienna 64, 65
-, Belvedere 65
-, Schönbrunn 64, 65
Vietnam 150–153
Viñales 273

Wadden Sea 57
Wrangel Island 135

Yellowstone 240, 241
Yemen 114, 115
Yosemite 236, 237

Zimbabwe 206, 207
Zion 242
Zurich 60

Index of images

Abbreviations:

A	Alamy
akg	akg-images
B	Bilderberg
C	Corbis
G	Getty Images
H	Huber
IB	The Image Bank
Ifa	ifa-Bilderteam
L	Laif
M	Mauritius
P	Premium

Cover: Island in the Indian Ocean, G/Neil Emmerson

Sorted from upper left to lower right

P.002-003 P/Winz; P.004-005 L/Fred Derwal; P.006-007 G/Justin Foulkes; P.008-009 G/Panoramic Images; P.010-011 G/Gary Yeowell; P.012 G/Harald Sund; P.012 G/Wilfried Krecichwost; P.012 A/Mikael Utterstrom; P.012 G/Altrendo Panoramic; P.012-013 Schapowalow/SIME; P.013 G/Arctic-Images; P.014 Erich Spiegelhalter; P.014-015 Erich Spiegelhalter; P.015 Bilderberg/Christophe Boisvieux; P.015 alimdi/Christian Handl; P.015 Erich Spiegelhalter; P.015 Schapowalow/Huber; P.016-017 Huber/Gräfenhain; P.017 G/Johner; P.017 G/Slow Images; P.018 G/Panoramic Images; P.018-019 L/Jörg Glaescher; P.019 Visum/Alfred Buellesbach; P.019 A/John Lens; P.019 G/Scott R Barbour; P.020 A/Imagebroker; P.020-021 G/Cesar Lucas Abreu; P.021 A/John Sparks; P.021 A/Blickwinkel; P.021 G/Jenny Pate; P.022-023 H.& D. Zielske; P.023 H.& D. Zielske; P.023 Caro/Ruffer; P.023 H.& D. Zielske; P.023 H.& D. Zielske; P.024 C/Reuters; P.024-025 A/Jim Zuckerman; P.025 Arco Images/NPL; P.026 Bilderberg/Wolfgang Fuchs; P.026 G/Kevin Schafer; P.026 G/Mike Caldwell; P.026-027 L/Hartmut Krinitz; P.028 A/Robert Harding Picture Library Ltd; P.028 A/Worldwide Picture Library; P.028 A/Worldwide Picture Library; P.028 A/Worldwide Picture Library; P.028 P; P.028-029 P; P.030 Ernst Wrba; P.030 C/Richard Cummins; P.030 Ifa/Panstock; P.030 P; P.031 G/Altrendo Panoramic; P.031 C/Farrell Grehan; P.031 ifa/Harris; P.031 ifa/Jon Arnold Images; P.031 P; P.032-033 G/Robert Harding; P.033 G/Harald Sund; P.034 Look/Sabine Lubenow; P.034 A/Imagina Photography; P.034 A/nagele-stock.com; P.034 P; P.035 L/Bertrand Rieger; P.036/037 H/Giovanni; P.037 Bilderberg/Dorothea Schmid; P.037 Bilderberg/Dorothea Schmid; P.037 Bilderberg/Dorothea Schmid; P.038 P; P.038/039 H/G. Simeone; P.039 ifa/Panstock; P.040 G/Travel Ink; P.040 G/Ruth Tomlinson; P.040/041 G/Ruth Tomlinson; P.041 ifa/panstock; P.041 Visum/Mark Bromhead; P.042 L/Frank Siemers; P.042 Look/Karl Johaentges; P.042 Schapowalow/Roy Rainford; P.042/043 P; P.043 ifa/Panstock; P.044 ifa/Diaf; P.044/045 G/Scott Stulberg; P.045 G/Art Wulfe; P.045 G/Jeremy Walker; P.045 G/Purestock; P.046 Jürgen Richter; P.046 G/Peter Adams; P.046 A/Peter Bowater; P.046 A/Look; P.046 A/PCL; P.046 G/Peter Higgins; P.046-047 Bilderberg/Frieder Blickle; P.047 L/; P.047 L/Raach; P.048 P; P.048-049 A/Look; P.049 G/Allan Baxter; P.049 G/Guy Vanderelst; P.049 G/Krzysztof Dydynsk; P.049 A/Peter Barritt; P.049 A/Look; P.049 G/Marco Cristofori; P.050 G/Frank Seifert; P.050 Jürgen Richter; P.050 G/Manfred Mehlig; P.050 H. & D. Zielske; P.050-051 G/Hans Strand; P.051 Martin Siepmann; P.051 A/Look; P.051 L/Gernot Huber; P.051 P; P.052 G/Guy Vanderelst; P.052 G/Guy Vanderelst; P.052 G/Guy Vanderelst; P.052-053 hemis/Bertrand Gardel; P.053 hemis/Thierry Borredon; P.053 C/John and Lisa Merrill; P.054 G/Siegfried Layda; P.054-055 G/David Sutherland; P.055 G/Peter Adams; P.056 L/Kreuels; P.056 Bilderberg/Simon Puschmann; P.056 G/Konrad Wothe; P.056-57 P; P.057 Look/Karl Johaentges; P.058 L/Biskup; P.058 ifa/Siebig; P.058-059 Look/Ingrid Firmhofer; P.059 Franz Marc Frei; P.059 Romeis; P.059 H. & D. Zielske; P.059 Schapowalow/Huber; P.060 G/Richard-Nowitz; P.060 Visum/Alfred Buellesbach; P.060 fotofinder/Dirk Renckhoff; P.060-061 Visum/Alfred Buellesbach; P.061 G/Panoramic Images; P.062-063 G/Jochen Schlenker; P.063 G/Panoramic Images; P.064 Carlos de Mello; P.064 Look/Jan Greune; P.064-065 Yadid Levy; P.065 L/Paul Hahn; P.065 L/Heeb; P.066 L/Caputo; P.066-067 A/Jon Arnold Images Ltd; P.067 alimdi.net / KFS; P.067 Schapowalow/Huber; P.068 Udo Bernhart; P.068 hemis/René Mattes; P.068-069 Visum/Gerhard Westrich; P.069 P; P.069 hemis/René Mattes; P.070 ifa/Alastor Photo; P.070-071 L/Max Galli; P.071 L/Max Galli; P.072 L/Max Galli; P.072 L/Le Figaro Magazine; P.072 A/art Kowalsky; P.072-073 ifa/Jon Arnold Images; P.073 G/Stone/travelpix Ltd.; P.074 G/Stone/Sylvian Grandadam; P.074 C/Mimmo Jodice; P.074 M; P.074-075 L/Celentano; P.075 Alcoceba, Felipe J.; P.075 Bilderberg/Walter Schmitz; P.075 L/Celentano; P.075 A/CuboImages srl; P.076 L/Max Galli; P.076 L/Top; P.076 G/Duane Rieder; P.076 G/Andrea Pistolesi; P.076-077 L/Max Galli; P.077 L/Reiner Harscher; P.077 L/Reiner Harscher; P.078 H/Schmid; P.078 M/Bibikow; P.078 Das Fotoarchiv/Müller; P.078-079 P; P.080 A/Bildagentur-online/McPhoto-PUM; P.080 A/Mc-Photo; P.080 A/Arco Images GmbH; P.080 A/Andreas Ehrhard; P.080 P; P.080 ifa/Tschanz; P.080-081 L/Florian Werner; P.081 P/Buss; P.082-083 G/Siegfried Layda; P.083 Bilderberg/Peter Ginter; P.083 Bilderberg/Tobias Gerber; P.084 Bilderberg/Frieder Blickle; P.084 Bilderberg/Franz Peterschroeder; P.084 Das Fotoarchiv/Markus Dlouhy; P.084-085 Bilderberg/Hans Madej; P.085 Bilderberg/Hans Madej; P.085 Bilderberg/Milan Horacek; P.085 Bilderberg/Frank Peterschroeder; P.086 L/Kristensen; P.086 L/Paul Hahn; P.086 L/Paul Hahn; P.086 L/Barth; P.086 Blumebild/Blume; P.086-087 H; P.087 L/Paul Hahn; P.087 L/Paul Hahn; P.087 ifa/Panstock; P.088 L/Iris Kuerschner; P.088-089 BA_Geduldig; P.090 L/Frank Heuer; P.090 L/Fulvio Zanettini; P.090-091 H/Johanna Huber; P.092 Martin Zwick; P.092-093 Martin Zwick; P.093 C/Philippe Caron; P.093 Visum/Woodfall; P.094 akg-images / Rainer Hackenberg; P.094 G/Johannes Eisele; P.094-095 C/Pete Saloutos; P.095 L/Pierre Adenis; P.095 L/Frank Heuer; P.096 Bilderberg/Angelika Jakob; P.096 G/A. Garozzo; P.096 A/David Crossland; P.096 G/Taxi/David Noton; P.096-097 ifa/Jon Arnold Images; P.098 P; P.098-099 A/Paul Carstairs; P.100 L/Bertrand Gardel; P.100-101 A/Jon Arnold Images Ltd; P.101 ifa/Jon Arnold Images; P.101 ifa/Jon Arnold Images; P.101 L/Toma Babovic; P.101 L/Frank Heuer; P.102 G/Fotoworld; P.102 M/Ferdinand Hollweck; P.102-103 G/Richard P.Durrance; P.103 Huber/Gräfenhain; P.104-105 mediacolors; P.106 Bilderberg/Alcoceba, Felipe J.; P.106-107 L/Max Galli; P.107 L/A. Neumann; P.107 ifa/Richard Nowitz; P.108 Bilderberg/Nomi Baumgartl; P.108 L/Naftali Hilger; P.108 L/Katja Hoffmann; P.108 ERIC MARTIN; P.108 L/Le Figaro Magazine; P.109 L/Axel Krause; P.109 Bilderberg/Klaus D. Francke; P.109 L/Amit Shabi; P.109 L/Le Figaro Magazine; P.109 ERIC MARTIN; P.109 Bilderberg/Felipe J. Alcoceba; P.109 Schapowalow/Atlantide; P.110 L/Hemis; P.110-111 L/Eid; P.111 Pictor; P.111 ifa/Aberham; P.112-113 C/Kazuyoshi Nomachi; P.113 C/Kazuyoshi Nomachi; P.113 L/Redux; P.113 Das Fotoarchiv; P.114 L/Thomas Grabka; P.114 L/Hemis; P.114 C/Michele Falzone; P.114-115 G/Michele Falzone; P.116 C/Walter Bibikow; P.116 G/Jochem D Wijnands; P.116 G/Alexander Hassenstein; P.116 L/Christian Heeb; P.116-117 M/Alamy; P.118 C/Tibor Bognár; P.118 C/Diego Lezama Orezzoli; P.118-119 C/Kazuyoshi Nomachi; P.119 Bilderberg/Christophe Boisvieux; P.119 Bilderberg/Christophe Boisvieux; P.119 L/Ulla Kimmig; P.119 L/Hoa-Qui; P.120 C/Kazuyoshi Nomachi; P.120 C/Michele Falzone; P.120-121 C/Dave Bartruff; P.122 G/Art Wolfe; P.122 G/Toshihiko Chinami; P.122-123 M/Alamy; P.124 Visum/Peter Schickert; P.124 G/Don Klumpp; P.124 A/David R. Frazier Photolibrary Inc; P.124-125 A/Roger Cracknell; P.125 L/Fred Derwal; P.125 A/Zach Holmes; P.125 A/Realimage; P.125 C/Macduff Everton; P.126 akg-images / Jean-Louis Nou; P.126 akg-images / Jean-Louis Nou; P.126 A/David Noton Photography; P.126-127 P; P.127 C/Blaine Harrington III; P.127 A/Jerome Horner; P.127 A/Douglas Lander; P.128 A/Gavin Hellier; P.128 A/PCL; P.128 Schapowalow/Robert Harding; P.128-129 C/Dave Bartruff; P.129 L/hemis; P.129 L; P.129 A/TNT Magazine; P.129 A/Craig Lovell; P.129 A/Martin Harvey; P.129 (FREELENS Pool) www.fnoxx.de; P.130 L/Conrad Piepenburg; P.130 Guido Alberto Rossi / TIPS; P.130 A/Travel shot; P.130-131 P; P.132 G/Dan Rafla; P.132 A/Robert Preston; P.133 P; P.134 C/Goodshoot; P.134 Wildlife; P.134 Wildlife; P.134 C/Yann Arthus-Bertrand; P.134-135 C/Wolfgang Kaehler; P.135 Juniors Tierbildarchiv; P.135 Blickwinkel/E. Hummel; P.135 C/Roger Tidman; P.135 C/Wolfgang Kaehler; P.136 C/Redlink; P.136 A/JLImages; P.136-137 C/Redlink; P.137 C/Liu Liqun; P.137 Panoramastock/Chu Young; P.138-139 Panoramastock/Chu Young; P.139 ifa/Montgomery; P.140-141 C/Paul Hardy; P.141 ifa/Jon Arnold Images; P.141 P/Pixtal; P.141 Jos Fuste Raga; P.141 Bruno Perousse; P.142 Panoramastock; P.142-143 L/Hauser; P.143 L/P P.Kristensen; P.144 C/Rob Howard; P.144 ifa/Montgomery; P.144 ifa/AP&F; P.144 ifa/Shashin Koubou; P.145 G/Martin Gray; P.146 Look/Hauke Dressler; P.146 G/Tom Bonaventure; P.146 G/Stone/Ehlers; P.148-149 Look/age fotostock; P.149 G/Stone; P.150-151 Bildagentur Huber/Graefenhain; P.151 G/Steven L. Raymer; P.151 L/Hemis; P.152 G/Wilfried Krecichwost; P.152-153 M/Alamy; P.153 G/ Lonely Planet Images/Andres Blomqvist; P.153 P/Pacific Stock; P.153 C/Steve Raymer; P.154-155 G/Steve Raymer; P.155 L/Hemispheres; P.155 L/Hemispheres; P.155 [Louis Meulstee]/Das Fotoarchiv; P.155 Cavalli,Angelo; P.156 C. & W. Kunth; P.156 C. & W. Kunth; P.156 C. & W. Kunth; P.156-157 L/Martin Krichner; P.157 G/Paul Chesley; P.157 ifa/Stadler; P.157 L/Markus Kirchgessner; P.157 Schapowalow/SIME; P.158 ifa/Roberto Massonori Arakaki; P.158-159 G/Paul Souders; P.159 C/Dave G. Houser; P.159 C/Nik Wheeler; P.160 G/Gerry Ellis; P.160 Wildlife; P.160 Michael J. Doolittle/Peter Arnold; P.160-161 A/Atmotu Images; P.161 A/Robbie Shone; P.161 Reinhard Dirscherl/WaterFrame; P.161 C/Robert Holmes; P.162 L/Clemens Emmler; P.162 Look/Kay Maeritz; P.162-163 L/Clemens Emmler; P.164-165 C/TSM/Faulkner; P.166 Geospace/Acres; P.166 ifa/Picture Finders; P.166 Don Fuchs; P.166-167 P; P.166-167 P/Image State; P.167 C/Gavriel Jecan; P.167 C/Joe Mc Donald; P.167 C/Jon Sparks; P.167 C/Joe McDonald; P.167 Okapia/Cyril Ruoso; P.168 Geospace/EDC; P.168 G/Chesley; P.168 P/Minden; P.168 P/Minden; P.168-169 Don Fuchs; P.170 Don Fuchs; P.170 Clemens Emmler; P.170 Blickwinkel; P.170-171 Ifa/Jon Arnold Images; P.172 Don Fuchs; P.172 Don Fuchs; P.172 C/Hans Strand; P.172 P; P.172-173 C/Yann Arthus-Bertrand; P.174 C/Steven Vidler; P.174 P/Minden/de Roy; P.174-175 Clemens Emmler; P.175 P/Image State/Allen; P.175 Tobias Hauser; P.176 P; P.176 L/Christian Heeb; P.176-177 Christian Heeb; P.177 Clemens Emmler; P.178 A/RH Picture Library Ltd.; P.178 C/Keren Su; P.178-179 C/Charles Lenars; P.180 C/Darrell Gulin; P.180-181 C/Yann Arthus-Bertrand; P.181 C/Jeff Flindt; P.182-183 P/Delphoto; P.184 G/Vision; P.184 C/C. Pawley; P.184 C/Christine Osborne; P.184-185 Huber/Ripani; P.185 L/Hilger; P.185 M/Jose Fuste Raga; P.185 L/Reporters; P.185 M/Rene Truffy; P.186 Bildagentur-online/Lescourret; P.186 © Deschamps / Andia.fr; P.186 Schapowalow/Atlantide; P.186-187 P; P.187 L/Frank Siemers; P.187 Huber/Ripani; P.187 L/Specht; P.188-189 A/Martin Norris; P.189 L/Michael Martin; P.189 ifa/Diaf; P.189 G/Sylvester Adams; P.190 L/Hemis; P.190 A/Pep Roig; P.190 ifa/Jean-Marc, Charles; P.190-191 C/Guenter Rossenbach; P.191 L/Peter Bialobrzeski; P.192 Clemens Emmler; P.192 L/Emmler; P.192 L/Markus Kirchgessner; P.192 L/Emmler; P.192 A/Gordon Sinclair; P.192 A/Gordon Sinclair; P.192-193 Clemens Emmler; P.193 Clemens Emmler; P.193 Michael Martin; P.193 L/Clemens Emmler; P.194 L/Arthur Selbach; P.194 L/Christian Heeb; P.194 G/Westmoreland; P.194 ifa/Alexandre; P.194 Das Fotoarchiv/Riedmiller; P.194-195 Look/Michael Martin; P.196 Ariadne Van Zandbergen; P.196 P/Boyer; P.196 G; P.196-197 Huber/Friedmar Damm; P.198 C/Nik Wheeler; P.198 Visum/Christoph Kohler; P.198 C/Yann Arthus-Bertrand; P.198-199 C/Yann Arthus-Bertrand; P.200 ifa/; P.200 P/Minden; P.200-201 C/Martin Harvey; P.201 G/Petersen; P.201 P/Minden; P.201 P/Stock Image; P.202 Pix/Minden/Lanting; P.202 G/Manoj Shah; P.202 G/Sean Russell; P.202 C/Rob Howard; P.202 C/Martin Harvey; P.202 Okapia; P.202-203 M; P.204-205 ifa/Aberham; P.205 C/Yann Arthus-Bertrand; P.206 G/Jake Wyman; P.206-207 G/Ian Cumming; P.207 L/Le Figaro Magazine; P.208 G/Paul Souders; P.208 P; P.208-209 G/Dave Hamman; P.210 C/Martin Harvey; P.210-211 C. & W. Kunth; P.211 P; P.212 Clemens Emmler; P.212 Clemens Emmler; P.212-213 A/Image State; P.213 P; P.213 Clemens Emmler; P.214 Clemens Emmler; P.214-215 ifa/Jon Arnold Images; P.215 Clemens Emmler; P.215 C/Dave G. Houser; P.216 Clemens Emmler; P.216 C/Bob Krist; P.216 Clemens Emmler; P.216 Das Fotoarchiv; P.216-217 Franz Marc Frei; P.217 Clemens Emmler; P.217 Clemens Emmler; P.218 C/Martin Harvey; P.218 C/Yann Arthus-Bertrand; P.218 G/Michael Melford; P.218 L/Gernot Huber; P.218 P/Minden; P.218-219 G/JH Pete Carmichel; P.220-221 L/Massimo Ripani; P.221 P/Transdia/Hänel; P.222-223 Huber/G. Simeone; P.223 Kurt Henseler; P.223 ifa; P.223 G/IB/Phillippe Burseiller; P.224-225 P/Stock Images; P.226 G/Panoramic Images; P.226-227 P/Yanagi; P.228 G/Joseph Squillante; P.228 P/Bunka; P.228-229 P/Orion Press; P.229 P/Schwabel; P.230 L/Christian Heeb; P.230 C/Rogers; P.230-231 L/Philippe Renault; P.232 C; P.232 C/Tim Thompson; P.232 P/Minden; P.232-233 C/Theo Allofs; P.233 P; P.233 ifa/Klaus Warter; P.234 P/Kosuge; P.234 P; P.234-235 G/Michele Falzone; P.235 P/Gilchrist; P.235 P/FirtsLight; P.235 Mauritius; P.236 G/Stone/Marc Muench; P.236 G/Don Smtih; P.236-237 G/Philip Schermeister; P.237 P/Sisk; P.238 P; P.238-239 G/Stone/George Diebold; P.240-241 P/Minden/Brandenburg; P.241 G/Tim Fritzharris; P.241 P/Roda; P.241 P/Minden; P.241 P/Minden/Brandenburg; P.242 Christian Heeb; P.242 Christian Heeb; P.242-243 L/Heeb; P.244 P/Schott; P.244-245 ifa/NovaStock; P.246-247 ifa/Krämer; P.247 C/James Randklev; P.247 P/Sisk; P.248 L/Christian Heeb; P.248 L/Christian Heeb; P.248 P/Schramm; P.248-249 P; P.249 L/Achim Multhaupt; P.249 L/Stefan falke; P.249 P; P.250-251 L/Martin Sasse; P.252 ifa/; P.252 L/Jörg Modrow; P.252 L/Jörg Modrow; P.252 P/Barbudo; P.252-253 ifa/Jon Arnold Images; P.253 Metzen,Wendell; P.253 L/REA; P.254 L/P S Kristensen; P.255 P/Mahlke; P.255 G/Norbert Wu; P.255 ifa/Gerhard Schulz; P.255 C/Joe McDonald; P.255 P/Mahlke; P.255 P/Pacific Stock; P.256-257 G/Art Wolfe; P.257 P; P.257 L/Heeb; P.257 P/Cavataio; P.258 L/Mayer; P.258 L/Gonzales; P.258 L/Mayer; P.258-259 G/Robert Frerck; P.258-259 P; P.259 L/Christian Heeb; P.259 L/Christian Heeb; P.259 A/geogphotos; P.259 A/Robert Fried; P.259 P/Roda; P.260 L/Bertrand Gardel; P.260 C/George Steinmetz; P.260-261 Huber/F.Damm; P.261 L/Christian Heeb; P.261 C/Jose Fuste Raga; P.261 © Mattes / Andia.fr; P.262 G/Picture Finders; P.262 G/Picture Finders; P.262-263 Marr; P.262-263 Marr; P.263 Ifa/Panstock; P.264 A/Images&Stories; P.264-265 Huber/Giovanni; P.266 L/Christian Heeb; P.266 C/Macduff Everton; P.266-267 L/Tophoven; P.267 C/Charles Lenars; P.268-269 L/Christian Heeb; P.269 G/Richard Ustinich; P.270 A/Michael Patrick O'Neill; P.270 L/Christian Heeb; P.270-271 Huber/Kiedrowski; P.271 L/Tobias Hauser; P.271 L/Tobias Hauser; P.271 A/Oyvind Martinsen; P.271 C/Kevin Schafer; P.271 A/Kevin Schafer; P.271 Kevin Schafer; P.272 L/Tobias Hauser; P.272 L/Tobias Hauser; P.272 L/Tobias Hauser; P.272 L/Tobias Hauser; P.272 M/age; P.272 L/Tobias Hauser; P.272-273 L/Tobias Hauser; P.274 G/Ken Fisher; P.274-275 A/Kevin Schafer; P.276 A/Wolfgang Kaehler; P.276 C/Yann Arthus-Bertrand; P.276-277 P; P.277 L/The NewYorkTimes; P.277 Look/Per-Andre Hoffmann; P.278 L/Tophoven; P.278-279 P; P.280-281 L/Gonzales; P.281 C/Pablo Corral Vega; P.282 C/Lehmann; P.282-283 G/Daniel Beltra; P.283 P; P.283 P; P.283 M; P.283 P/Pecha; P.283 M/Wendler; P.284 G/Cassio Vasconcellos; P.284 L/Christian Heeb; P.284 G/Richard T. Nowitz; P.284-285 G/John Lamb; P.286-287 A/Tibor Bognar; P.287 Premium; P.288 Woodhouse; P.288 C/Julie Houck; P.288 P/Japack; P.288-289 G/Andrew Geiger; P.289 C/Hubert Stadler; P.289 C/Pablo Corral Vega; P.289 C/Pablo Corral Vega; P.290 C/Tony West; P.290 C/Hubert Stadler; P.290-291 C/Galen Rowell; P.291 P/Panoramic Images; P.292 Woodhouse; P.292 P/Hummel; P.292-293 G/Ed Darack; P.293 C/Hubert Stadler; P.293 C/Hubert Stadler; P.293 C/Hubert Stadler; P.294-295 L/Marcel Malherbe; P.295 Huber; P.295 MASSIMO RIPANI; P.296-297 Schapowalow / Huber; P.297 Huber/Bernhart; P.297 L/Gonzales; P.298-299 Look/Michael Boyny; P.300-301 P/Hummel; P.301 P/Minden/WINFRIED WISNIEWSKI

MONACO BOOKS is an imprint of Kunth Verlag Gmbh& Co. KG
© Kunth Verlag Gmbh& Co. KG, Munich, 2015
English edition:
Translation: Sylvia Goulding, Katherine Taylor

For distribution please contact:
Monaco Books
c/o Kunth Verlag Gmbh & Co. KG, Königinstr.11
80539 München, Germany
Tel: +49 / 89/45 80 20 23
Fax: +49 / 89/ 45 80 20 21
info@kunth-verlag.de

www.monacobooks.com
www.kunth-verlag.de

Printed in Slovenia

All rights reserved. Reproduction, storage in a data processing system, or transmission by electronic means, by photocopying or similar, is only possible with the express permission of the copyright owner.
All facts have been researched with the greatest possible care to the best of our knowledge and belief. However, the editors and publishers can accept no responsibility for any inaccuracies or incompleteness of the details provided.
The publishers are pleased to receive any information or suggestions for improvement.

The World's greatest places
910.202 WORLD   **31057012331420**

WGRL-HQ NONFIC
31057012331420
910.202 WORLD
Monaco Books.
World's greatest places :
the most amazing travel dest

03/16